FOUNDATIONS A

READING
EXPLORER

THIRD EDITION

BECKY TARVER-CHASE

DAVID BOHLKE

NATIONAL GEOGRAPHIC
LEARNING

Australia · Brazil · Mexico · Singapore · United Kingdom · United States

National Geographic Learning,
a Cengage Company

**Reading Explorer Foundations Split A
Third Edition**

Becky Tarver-Chase and David Bohlke

Publisher: Andrew Robinson

Executive Editor: Sean Bermingham

Senior Development Editor: Christopher Street

Director of Global Marketing: Ian Martin

Heads of Regional Marketing:

  Charlotte Ellis (Europe, Middle East and Africa)

  Kiel Hamm (Asia)

  Irina Pereyra (Latin America)

Product Marketing Manager: Tracy Bailie

Senior Production Controller: Tan Jin Hock

Associate Media Researcher: Jeffrey Millies

Art Director: Brenda Carmichael

Operations Support: Hayley Chwazik-Gee

Manufacturing Planner: Mary Beth Hennebury

Composition: MPS North America LLC

Foundations Split A with Online Workbook:
ISBN-13: 978-0-357-12461-1

Foundations Split A:
ISBN-13: 978-0-357-12369-0

National Geographic Learning
200 Pier Four Blvd
Boston, MA 02210
USA

Locate your local office at **international.cengage.com/region**

Visit National Geographic Learning online at **ELTNGL.com**
Visit our corporate website at **www.cengage.com**

Printed in China
Print Number: 01 Print Year: 2019

CONTENTS

Scope and Sequence		4
Introduction		6
Unit 1:	**Mysteries**	7
Unit 2:	**Eating Extremes**	21
Unit 3:	**Cool Jobs**	35
Unit 4:	**Shipwrecks**	49
Unit 5:	**Science Investigators**	63
Unit 6:	**Plants and Trees**	75
Credits and Acknowledgments		173
Glossary / Exam Question Type Index		175
Tips for Effective Reading		176

SCOPE AND SEQUENCE

UNIT	THEME	READING	VIDEO
1	Mysteries	A: A Mysterious Visitor B: The Lost City of Atlantis	Moon Mystery
2	Eating Extremes	A: The World of Speed Eating B: The Hottest Chilies	Science of Taste
3	Cool Jobs	A: Digging for the Past B: Getting the Shot	Right Dog for the Job
4	Shipwrecks	A: I've Found the Titanic! B: My Descent to the Titanic	An Ancient Shipwreck
5	Science Investigators	A: The Disease Detective B: At the Scene of a Crime	The Flu Virus
6	Plants and Trees	A: Planting for the Planet B: Fatal Attraction	Giants of the Forest

ACADEMIC SKILLS

READING SKILL	VOCABULARY BUILDING	CRITICAL THINKING
A: Scanning **B:** Skimming	**A:** Word usage: *pass* and *past* **B:** Word forms of *sink* and *strike*	**A:** Applying Ideas **B:** Synthesizing Information
A: Identifying the Parts of a Passage **B:** Pronoun Reference	**A:** Collocations with *argue* **B:** Collocations with *painful*	**A:** Justifying Opinions **B:** Applying Ideas
A: Dealing with New Vocabulary (1)—Using a Dictionary **B:** Understanding Suffixes	**A:** Collocations with *get* **B:** Word forms of *pay, cost,* and *spend*	**A:** Evaluating Advice **B:** Personalizing; Synthesizing Information
A: Identifying a Paragraph's Main Idea **B:** Recognizing Compound Subjects and Objects	**A:** Word usage: *agree* **B:** Synonyms for *totally*	**A:** Evaluating Arguments **B:** Evaluating Ideas; Justifying Ideas
A: Identifying the Purpose of a Paragraph **B:** Inferring Meaning	**A:** Suffix *-ous* **B:** Word forms of *possible*	**A:** Applying Ideas **B:** Evaluating Evidence; Sythesizing Information
A: Creating a Timeline of Events **B:** Understanding a Process	**A:** Word forms with *-ation* **B:** Collocations with *difference*	**A:** Justifying Opinions **B:** Applying Ideas

READING EXPLORER brings the world to your classroom.

With *Reading Explorer* you learn about real people and places, experience the world, and explore topics that matter.

What you'll see in the Third Edition:

Real-world stories give you a better understanding of the world and your place in it.

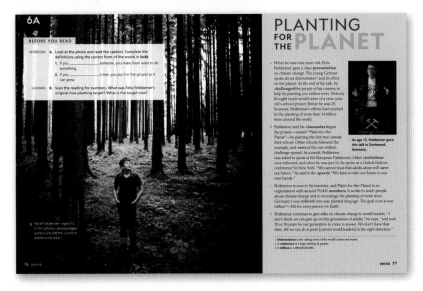

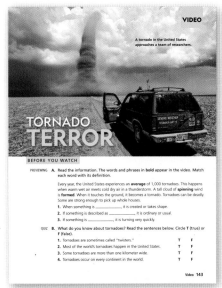

National Geographic Videos expand on the unit topic and give you a chance to apply your language skills.

Reading Skill and **Reading Comprehension** sections provide the tools you need to become an effective reader.

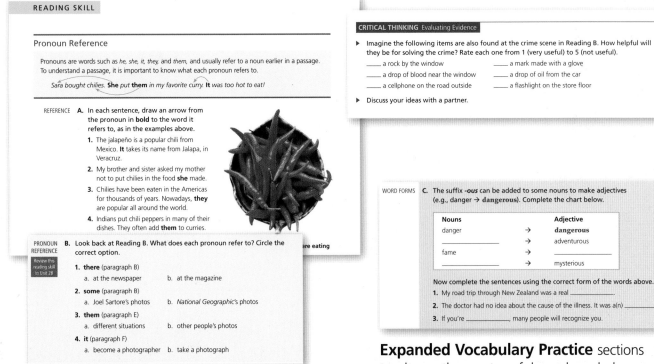

Expanded Vocabulary Practice sections teach you the most useful words and phrases needed for academic reading.

MYSTERIES

California's "sailing stones" were once a mystery. We now know that the rocks are moved by strong winds when the ground is icy.

WARM UP

Discuss these questions with a partner.

1. Read the caption. How do the rocks move?

2. Do you think there are things that science cannot explain? If so, give an example.

BEFORE YOU READ

DEFINITIONS **A.** Look at the image and read the caption. Complete the definitions using the words in **bold**.

   1. _____: scientists who study objects in space
   2. _____: a rock that moves through space

SKIMMING **B.** Skim the passage. According to some scientists, what else could 'Oumuamua be?

⌄ An artist's drawing of 'Oumuamua—a strangely shaped object that passed by Earth. **Astronomers** are not sure if it was an **asteroid**, or something else altogether.

A MYSTERIOUS VISITOR

A In October 2017, astronomers in Hawaii saw something surprising. A **strange** object was moving through the solar system. They had seen many asteroids before, but this was something different. It was long and **thin**—like a cucumber. The object's **speed** and direction also showed something surprising. This was an interstellar[1] object—the first ever seen.

B The object was named 'Oumuamua—Hawaiian for "visitor from afar." Nobody is sure exactly what it is. The simplest idea is that 'Oumuamua is a strangely shaped piece of rock. Perhaps it was **knocked** out of a far-off star system. However, astronomers saw that its speed increased after **passing** the sun. Some scientists therefore suggest a different theory.

C "'Oumuamua could be a piece of alien **technology**," says Professor Abraham Loeb from Harvard University. Loeb believes this could explain the object's long, thin shape, and also its change in speed. **Maybe** 'Oumuamua was a spaceship that came to **explore** our solar system. "All possibilities should be considered," says Loeb.

Professor Abraham Loeb suggested that 'Oumuamua could be an alien spaceship.

D 'Oumuamua can no longer be seen from Earth. But astronomers continue to study the information they got from it. It is still not clear if the object was a large rock, or something else altogether. 'Oumuamua will likely be a mystery for many years to come.

---

1 If an object is described as **interstellar**, it has traveled between different stars.

'Oumuamua: What We Know

- Entered the inner solar system in August 2017 **❶**. Possibly came from a star system **25 light years** from our sun—a **600,000-year** journey.

- Reached a top speed of **315,800 km/h**—more than **250** times the speed of sound—as it passed the sun **❷**.

- First seen by astronomers in October 2017 when it was **33,000,000 km** from Earth—about **85** times further than our moon **❸**.

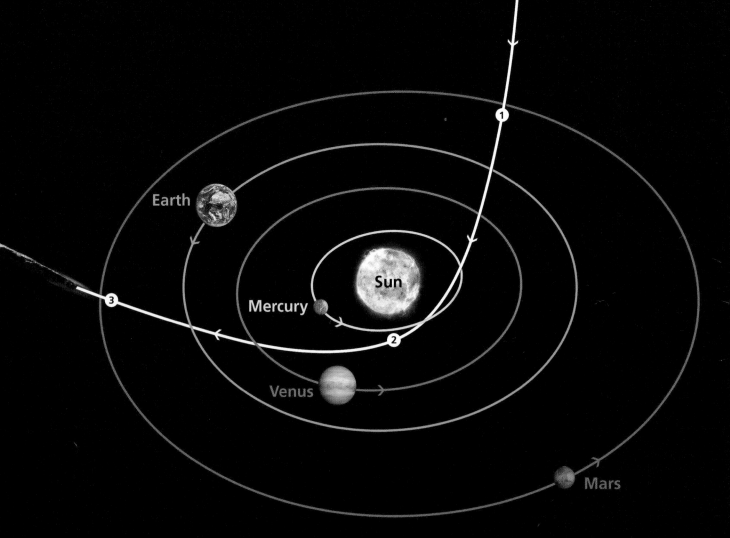

A. Choose the best answer for each question.

GIST

1. What is the reading mainly about?

    a. new technology to help scientists find asteroids

    b. the largest asteroid ever seen by scientists

    c. a mysterious object that passed by Earth

DETAIL

2. What did scientists learn from studying 'Oumuamua's speed and direction?

    a. It came from another star system.

    b. It was possible it could hit the Earth.

    c. It was an asteroid.

DETAIL

3. What is NOT given as a reason why 'Oumuamua could be an alien spaceship?

    a. the object's size and shape

    b. the object's change in speed

    c. the object's color

VOCABULARY

4. In paragraph C, what does *considered* mean?

    a. explained in detail

    b. thought about carefully

    c. chosen from a list

INFERENCE

5. According to the infographic on page 10, when was 'Oumuamua first seen from Earth?

    a. as it entered the inner solar system

    b. just before it passed the sun

    c. after it passed the sun

Scientists believe 'Oumuamua is spinning end-over-end as it travels through space.

SUMMARIZING

B. Complete the summary with the phrases in the box. One is extra.

a. alien technology	b. a cucumber	c. another star system
d. a rock	e. its speed and direction	f. our solar system

In October 2017, astronomers saw a strange object that was shaped like [1]_____.

By studying [2]_____, the scientists realized that the object had come from [3]_____.

The object was called 'Oumuamua. Most scientists think it was just [4]_____.

However, others—such as Abraham Loeb—have suggested it could be a piece of [5]_____.

Scanning

You scan a text when you want to find specific information. When you scan, you only look for the information you want. You don't read the rest of the text. For example, for the question *What does 'Oumuamua mean in Hawaiian?*, look through the text for the words *'Oumuamua* and *Hawaiian*, and possibly quotation marks (" ").

SCANNING **A.** Look back at Reading A. Find and underline these words in the passage as quickly as you can.

1. Hawaii
2. surprising
3. theory
4. alien
5. solar system
6. likely

SCANNING **B.** Read the questions below. Think about what answers you need to look for. Then scan Reading A and the infographic on page 10, and write the answers.

1. When did astronomers first see 'Oumuamua? _____
2. What does 'Oumuamua mean in Hawaiian? _____
3. When did 'Oumuamua's speed increase? _____
4. What is Abraham Loeb's job? _____
5. Where does Abraham Loeb work? _____
6. When did 'Oumuamua enter the inner solar system? _____
7. What was 'Oumuamua's top speed? _____
8. How far was 'Oumuamua from Earth when it was first seen? _____

CRITICAL THINKING Applying Ideas   What extra information about 'Oumuamua would be useful to help scientists solve the mystery? Note some ideas below. Then discuss with a partner.

_____

_____

> 'Oumuamua was first spotted by astronomers at the Haleakalā Observatory in Hawaii.

DEFINITIONS **A.** Read the information. Match each word in **red** with its definitions.

Crop Circles

A farmer wakes up to find something very **strange**. Someone, or **maybe** some*thing*, has made unusual shapes in his field by pushing down his crops.[1] The shapes can only be seen from the sky. These are called crop circles.

Some people think that aliens make crop circles when they land their spaceships. However, it seems clear that they are made by people. The **technology** to make them is simple—just a rope and different sizes of wood to make thick or **thin** lines.

Some people make crop circles so others will believe in aliens. Other people make them just for fun.

∧ **A crop circle is made by pushing crops down, leaving empty spaces in the field.**

---

1 **Crops** are plants grown in large amounts.

1. _____: hard to understand or explain

2. _____: perhaps; possibly

3. _____: not wide or thick

4. _____: the use of science and machines to do things

DEFINITIONS **B.** Match the two parts of each definition.

1. If you move at high **speed**, •   • a. you hit it.

2. If you **knock** something,   •   • b. you go very fast.

3. If you **pass** a place,   •   • c. you learn more about it.

4. When you **explore** a place, •   • d. you do not stop there.

WORD USAGE **C.** The past tense of the verb **pass** (*passed*) is sometimes confused with the preposition *past*. Complete the sentences by circling the correct words.

1. Scientists saw a large asteroid moving *past* / *passed* Earth.

2. I *passed* / *past* by the supermarket on my way home, so I bought some bread.

3. My friend just walked *passed* / *past* me and didn't stop to chat.

4. 'Oumuamua reached its top speed as it *past* / *passed* the sun.

BEFORE YOU READ

PREVIEWING   **A.** Look at the picture and read the caption. Who wrote the story of Atlantis? What happened to the island?

SCANNING   **B.** Quickly scan the passage on the next page. Remember that names of people and places usually start with capital letters.

Review this reading skill in Unit 1A

     1. What names of people can you find? Underline them.

     2. What names of places are mentioned? Circle them.

THE LOST CITY OF ATLANTIS

▽ **Long ago, the Greek writer Plato wrote about Atlantis—an island that disappeared into the sea.**

A   Most people have heard the story of the **lost** city of Atlantis. But is any part of the story true?

B   Over two thousand years ago, the Greek writer Plato wrote about Atlantis, an island in the Atlantic Ocean. The island's people were very rich. They built a big city with many great buildings. But the people became greedy—they had many things, but they still wanted more. So the gods became angry. Earthquakes[1] and large waves began to **strike** the island. **Finally**, Atlantis **sank** into the sea.

C   Many explorers have looked for Atlantis. In 2004, explorer Robert Sarmast **reported** finding the remains[2] of a city under the sea near Cyprus. However, Sarmast and other scientists later realized the structures he found under the sea were **natural**, not man-made. Mark Adams, author of the 2016 book *Meet Me in Atlantis* believes the city was in Morocco. Plato wrote about red and black stone circles around the city. Adams found similar red and black stones in the desert there, very near the Atlantic Ocean.

D   Most people, however, think Atlantis is simply a story. The **purpose** of the story may be to teach people not to be greedy. Richard Ellis also wrote a book about Atlantis in 1999. He says "there is not a **piece** of solid evidence"[3] for a real Atlantis.

E   So was the island real or not? We only know one thing: The mystery of Atlantis will be with us for a long time.

---

1   An **earthquake** is the shaking of the ground caused by movement of the Earth.
2   The **remains** of something are the parts that are left after most of it is gone.
3   **Evidence** is anything that makes you believe that something is true.

A. Choose the best answer for each question.

GIST

1. What could be another title for the reading?

a. Atlantis Sinks
b. Is Atlantis Real?
c. I Found Atlantis!

SEQUENCE

2. What happened after Robert Sarmast said he found Atlantis?

a. He wrote a book about his findings.
b. Richard Ellis said that Atlantis was not real.
c. He found out the structures were not man-made.

MAIN IDEA

3. What is the main idea of paragraph C?

a. Scientists believe Atlantis is just a story.
b. Explorers found a city under the sea near Morocco.
c. People have looked for Atlantis, but no one has found it.

△ **The story of Atlantis was first written down in Plato's *Dialogues* in 360 B.C.**

DETAIL

4. Why does Mark Adams believe Atlantis could be in Morocco?

a. He discovered the remains of houses in the ocean there.
b. He found colored stones similar to ones described by Plato.
c. He found a map that showed Atlantis's location in the Atlantic Ocean.

PARAPHRASING

5. In paragraph D, which sentence is closest in meaning to *"there is not a piece of solid evidence"* for a real Atlantis?

a. There is only one reason to believe the Atlantis story is true.
b. The story of Atlantis is made up of many small pieces.
c. There is nothing to make us believe the Atlantis story is true.

SCANNING

Review this reading skill in Unit 1A

B. Write short answers to the questions below. Use words from the passage for each answer.

1. When did Plato write about Atlantis? _____

2. When did Robert Sarmast report finding the remains of a city? _____

3. What was the title of Mark Adams's book? _____

4. Which author thinks Atlantis is just a story? _____

Skimming

You skim when you look quickly at the whole reading to see what it is about. You do not read every word. Instead, look at the title, headings, photos, and captions. Read the first line of each paragraph, and quickly read the conclusion.

SKIMMING OR SCANNING

A. Look at these reasons for reading. For each reason, should you skim or scan? Check (✓) the correct boxes.

	Skim	Scan
1. to see if a story is funny or serious	☐	☐
2. to find the names of countries mentioned	☐	☐
3. to find a quote (" ") by a scientist	☐	☐
4. to see how the author feels about a topic	☐	☐

SKIMMING

B. Quickly skim the passage below. What is it mainly about? Circle the correct option.

a. A diver who found Atlantis in the Pacific Ocean

b. A scientist who believes he has found a lost land near Japan

c. A strange structure that was found in a Japanese city

∧ **A diver explores the strange steplike structures in the waters near the Yonaguni Islands.**

The Lost Continent in the Pacific Ocean

People believe that thousands of years ago the lost continent of Mu sank because of an earthquake. Today, no one knows if there really was a place called Mu, or where it was.

However, Professor Masaaki Kimura thinks he knows where the remains of Mu are. He believes they are near the Yonaguni Islands of Japan. Kimura thinks the strange structures he has found were made by people. Some other researchers don't think so. No one is sure, but the research continues.

CRITICAL THINKING Synthesizing Information   Which mystery do you think will be more difficult to solve: Atlantis or 'Oumuamua? Why? Note your ideas below. Then discuss with a partner.

_____

_____

_____

VOCABULARY PRACTICE

DEFINITIONS **A.** Read the information. Match each word in **red** with its definition.

Some people believe the Greek island of Santorini is the likely location for the **lost** city of Atlantis. The two are similar in several ways.

Plato described Atlantis as being in the shape of a circle. In the past, Santorini was also circular. However, the island was **struck** by earthquakes and nearly destroyed by a volcano, causing parts of the island to **sink**. There were also people living in cities on Santorini for thousands of years.

∧ **The Greek island of Santorini viewed from above**

There are, however, important differences. First of all, the dates in Plato's writing do not match with events on Santorini. Plato also said Atlantis was in the Atlantic Ocean, but Santorini is in the Mediterranean Sea. And **finally**, the sizes of the two islands are very different. Atlantis was described as very large, but Santorini is small.

1. _____: lastly, in the end

2. _____: unable to be found

3. _____: suddenly hit

4. _____: to move slowly downwards, often in water.

COMPLETION **B.** Complete the sentences. Circle the correct options.

1. Something **natural** is *made / not made* by humans.

2. A **piece** of something is *all / part* of it.

3. To find out the **purpose** of something, you should ask *"Where?" / "Why?"*

4. When you **report** something, you *don't tell / tell* others about it.

WORD FORMS **C.** Many verbs, such as **sink** and **strike**, have irregular past forms. Complete the sentences using the words in the box.

sink	sank	strike	struck

1. Last night, large waves _____ the side of the ship.

2. If you drop coins in water, they _____.

3. Earthquakes often _____ in countries along the Pacific.

4. Sadly, their small boat _____ in the storm.

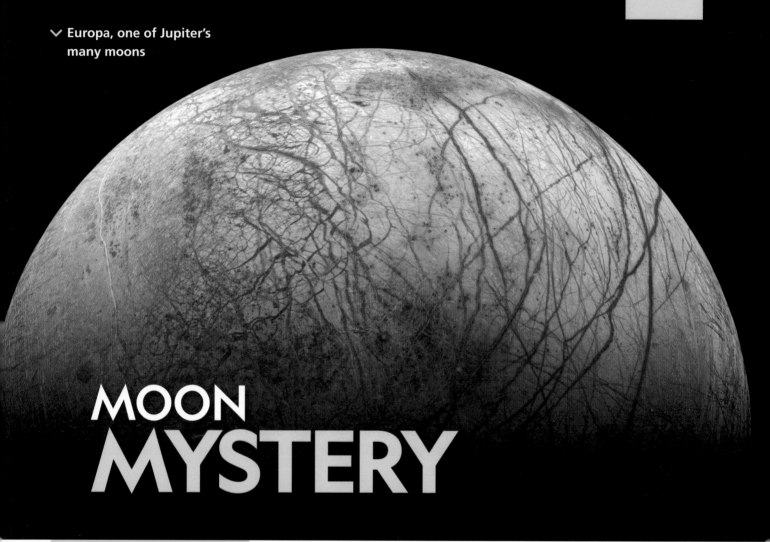

∨ Europa, one of Jupiter's many moons

MOON MYSTERY

BEFORE YOU WATCH

PREVIEWING **A.** Read the information. The words in **bold** appear in the video. Complete the definitions with the correct form of each word.

For many years, scientists have searched for life in space. Spacecrafts have been sent to every planet in the solar system, and robots have landed on the **surfaces** of Mars and Venus. So far, nothing has been found. Many believe, however, that the best places to look for life might not be planets at all. Europa—one of Jupiter's many moons—is thought to have **conditions** where life may **exist**. Whether it does or not remains a mystery for now.

1. If something ＿＿＿＿＿＿＿＿, it stays alive.

2. The ＿＿＿＿＿＿＿＿ of something is the outside part of it.

3. The ＿＿＿＿＿＿＿＿ of a place include things like its temperature or weather.

DISCUSSION **B.** Why do you think scientists believe there might be life on Europa? What conditions might exist there? Note your ideas. Then discuss with a partner.

＿＿＿＿＿＿＿＿＿＿＿＿＿＿＿＿＿＿＿＿＿＿＿＿＿＿＿＿＿＿＿＿＿＿

GIST **A.** Watch the video. Why do scientists believe Europa is a good place to look for life? Choose the correct answer.

a. ☐ It may have an ocean beneath its surface.

b. ☐ Its surface temperature is similar to Earth's.

c. ☐ It is a similar size to Earth's moon.

DETAILS **B.** Watch the video again. Complete the notes.

Discovered by Galileo in ¹_____

Europa

Future missions may send a(n) ⁵_____ to Europa.

Slightly smaller than ²_____

Surface covered in ³_____

Life has been found on ⁴_____ in similar conditions.

CRITICAL THINKING Applying Ideas   Consider what you know about the conditions on Europa. If scientists do find life there, what do you think it will look like? Note your ideas or draw a picture. Explain your ideas to a partner.

_____

_____

_____

VOCABULARY REVIEW

Do you remember the meanings of these words? Check (✓) the ones you know. Look back at the unit and review any words you're not sure of.

Reading A

☐ explore   ☐ knock   ☐ maybe   ☐ pass

☐ speed   ☐ strange   ☐ technology*   ☐ thin

Reading B

☐ finally*   ☐ lost   ☐ natural   ☐ piece

☐ purpose   ☐ report   ☐ sink   ☐ strike

* Academic Word List

EATING
EXTREMES

Cooks prepare a 2-kilometer-long pizza as part of a world record attempt in Naples, Italy.

WARM UP

Discuss these questions with a partner.

1. Have you ever eaten any unusual food?

2. What's the hottest (spiciest) food you've ever eaten?

The Nathan's Famous Hot Dog Eating Contest is held every year on the Fourth of July in New York, United States.

BEFORE YOU READ

PREVIEWING **A.** Look at the photo and read the caption. What kind of competition is it? Where and when does it take place?

PREDICTING **B.** How many hot dogs do you think one person can eat in 10 minutes? Discuss your ideas with a partner. Scan the passage on pages 23–24 to check your ideas.

THE WORLD OF SPEED EATING

A Competitive eating—or speed eating—is **exactly** what its name suggests. Contestants[1] eat as much as they can, usually within a time limit. Eating competitions can involve **various** foods—pizza, pies, ice cream, chili peppers. They can also offer large prizes to the winners.

The Biggest Competition

B The world's largest competitive eating event is Nathan's Famous Hot Dog Eating Contest. The event is held every Fourth of July in Brooklyn, New York. According to legend,[2] this tradition began over a hundred years ago. Four immigrants[3] were **arguing** about who loved their new country the most. Finally, they **worked out** a way to decide. They would see who could eat the most of a famous American food—the hot dog. James Mullen, an Irish immigrant, won by eating 13 hot dogs in 12 minutes. Nathan's Fourth of July **tradition** was born.

---

1 A **contestant** is someone who takes part in a competition.

2 A **legend** is a traditional story that may or may not be true.

3 An **immigrant** is someone who has left one country to live in another.

Eating Champions

C The current champion* of the contest is Joey Chestnut. Chestnut—an American—also holds the world **record** for hot dog eating—74 in less than 10 minutes. That's just over 8 seconds per hot dog. For many years, the Nathan's Contest champion was Takeru Kobayashi from Japan. He is smaller and lighter than Chestnut, and doesn't look like an eating champion. However, he holds many world records for eating different types of food.

Bad Taste or Just Sport?

D Not everybody thinks competitive eating is a good thing. It can be **unhealthy** for the contestants, and many people in the world are going hungry. Kobayashi first won the event in 2001 when he was 23 years old. So are eating competitions in bad taste? For competitive eaters, it's a sport like any other. As Kobayashi says, "Food fighters … think of themselves as **athletes**."

* as of 2018

KOBAYASHI'S WORLD RECORDS

- **15½** pizzas in **12** minutes
- **150** rice balls in **30** minutes
- **93** hamburgers in **8** minutes
- **159** tacos in **10** minutes
- **13** grilled cheese sandwiches in **1** minute

◁ "I know I have a special stomach," says Takeru Kobayashi.

A. Choose the best answer for each question.

GIST

1. What is the reading mainly about?

    a. the history of hot dogs in the United States

    b. the career of a famous competitive eater

    c. eating competitions and the people who take part

PURPOSE

2. What is the purpose of paragraph B?

    a. to give details about a famous competitive eating event

    b. to explain how competitive eaters can eat so quickly

    c. to describe the dangers of competitive eating

DETAIL

3. What is NOT true about Joey Chestnut?

    a. He is smaller than Takeru Kobayashi.

    b. He has won Nathan's Famous Hot Dog Eating Contest.

    c. He broke the world record for hot dog eating.

PARAPHRASING

4. In paragraph D, which word could replace *in bad taste*?

    a. wrong

    b. dangerous

    c. exciting

⌃ **Joey Chestnut is one of the world's most successful speed eaters.**

INFERENCE

5. Which of the following would Takeru Kobayashi most likely say?

    a. "Competitive eating is just a fun hobby for me. Winning isn't important."

    b. "I see competitive eating as a sport, and I always try my best."

    c. "Eating so much food is unhealthy. Eating competitions should be stopped."

SCANNING

Review this reading skill in Unit 1A

B. Scan the passage for the names in the box. Match each person (a–c) with the sentence that describes them. Each person may be used more than once.

a. James Mullen	b. Joey Chestnut	c. Takeru Kobayashi

1. _____ helped start the tradition of hot dog eating contests.

2. _____ won the 2018 Nathan's Famous Hot Dog Eating Contest.

3. _____ was born in Ireland.

4. _____ holds a record for eating hamburgers.

Identifying the Parts of a Passage

A reading passage can have several parts. Look at every part to get a complete understanding of the passage. This is very useful when previewing a passage or predicting what it contains.

The **title** is a kind of **heading**. It tells you what the whole text is about.

Photos and **illustrations** show information visually.

Subheadings above **paragraphs** tell you what they are about.

Footnotes give definitions of difficult vocabulary.

Maps show you where in the world a place is.

Captions explain the pictures.

Sidebars give additional information about the topic.

IDENTIFYING **A.** Look back at Reading A. Which parts of a passage are used there? Check (✓) the parts you can find.

☐ a title ☐ photos ☐ subheadings ☐ a map

☐ illustrations ☐ a sidebar ☐ captions ☐ footnotes

SCANNING **B.** Look back at the reading again. Answer the questions below.

1. What is the title of the reading? _____
2. How many paragraphs are there in the main text? _____
3. Does every photo have a caption? _____
4. How many footnotes are there? _____
5. Whose records are in the sidebar? _____

CRITICAL THINKING Justifying Opinions Discuss with a partner. The author asks if some eating contests are "in bad taste." What do you think? Would you ever enter one?

VOCABULARY PRACTICE

DEFINITIONS **A.** Complete the information. Circle the correct options.

   1. An example of an **athlete** is a *singer* / *soccer player*.

   2. People sometimes **argue** when they *agree* / *disagree* about something.

   3. When you **work out** something, you *find the answer* / *tell a story*.

   4. If something is **unhealthy**, it is *bad* / *good* for you.

COMPLETION **B.** Complete the information using the words in the box. Two words are extra.

argue	athlete	exactly	records	tradition	various

Every year, the small Czech town of Vizovice holds a festival to celebrate the plums grown in the area. The festival has a long ¹_____, recently celebrating its 50th year. One of its most popular events is a plum dumpling eating contest.

In 2017, American Patrick Bertoletti won the contest. He ate ²_____ 198 dumplings in one hour. Bertoletti has held ³_____ other world ⁴_____ in speed eating. He won the 2015 Wing Bowl when he ate an amazing 444 chicken wings in just 26 minutes.

△ **Patrick Bertoletti shows off his Wing Bowl championship ring after winning the 2015 event.**

COLLOCATIONS **C.** The prepositions in the box can be used with the verb **argue**. Complete the sentences using the correct prepositions.

about	for	with

   1. The people in the eating contest argued _____ the rules.

   2. The customer argued _____ the server because his food came out cold.

   3. The kitchen workers argued _____ more money because they make very little.

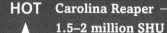

HOT Carolina Reaper
1.5–2 million SHU

Trinidad Moruga Scorpion
1,463,700 SHU

Naga Jolokia 1,041,427 SHU

Dorset Naga 923,000 SHU

Tabasco 190,542 SHU

Thai Chili 60,000 SHU

Jalapeño 5,500 SHU

MILD Sweet Bell Pepper 0 SHU

⌃ Scientists use Scoville heat units (SHU)
to rate a chili pepper's "heat" level.

BEFORE YOU READ

TRUE OR FALSE **A.** Look at the information above. Is each sentence below true or false?
Circle **T** (true) or **F** (false).

1. The Trinidad Moruga Scorpion is hotter than the Dorset Naga. **T   F**
2. A chili pepper that measures 5,000 SHU is very hot. **T   F**
3. Tabasco peppers are hotter than jalapeños. **T   F**
4. Sweet bell peppers have a very high SHU level. **T   F**

SCANNING **B.** In Assam, India, a woman named Anandita Dutta Tamuly likes to eat very
hot chilies. Quickly scan the passage on the next page. Which of the chilies
above is she famous for eating?

Review this
reading skill
in Unit 1A

THE HOTTEST CHILIES

A You may have experienced the feeling. Your mouth feels like it's on fire. Your eyes start to water. You just ate one of nature's hottest foods—the chili pepper!

B Chili peppers, also called chilies, are found in **dishes** around the world. They are in dishes like Indian curries, Thai tom yum soup, and Mexican enchiladas. Chilies come from the capsicum **plant**. They are "hot" because they **contain** something called *capsaicin*.

C Capsaicin is very good for your **health**. It helps you **breathe** better, and it may even help keep you **fit**. Capsaicin makes you feel less **hungry**. It also makes your body burn more calories.[1]

D We can measure the heat of chilies in units called Scoville heat units (SHU). The world's hottest chili is the Carolina Reaper. It sometimes measures up to 2 million SHU!

E Eating a hot chili can be **painful**, but some people love to eat them. Anandita Dutta Tamuly, a woman from Assam, India, became famous for eating chilies. She ate 51 hot peppers in just two minutes! The peppers were Naga Jolokia ("ghost peppers"). They grow in Assam and are the third-hottest chilies in the world.

F "I found eating chilies was a great way to stay healthy," says Tamuly. She began eating chilies when she was a child. She eats chilies when she is sick, too. "Every time I have a cold or flu, I just eat some chilies and I feel better. To be honest, I barely notice them now."

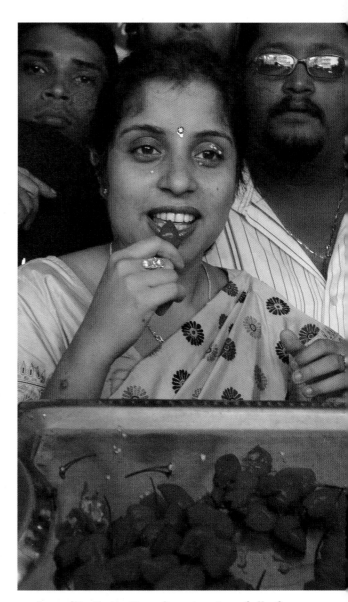

⌃ **Anandita Dutta Tamuly eats a tray full of Naga Jolokia, or "ghost peppers."**

---

1 **Calories** are units used to measure the energy value of food.

A. Choose the best answer for each question.

GIST

1. What is the reading mainly about?

    a. how to eat very hot chili peppers

    b. facts about hot chili peppers

    c. ideas for cooking using chili peppers

PURPOSE

2. What is the purpose of paragraph C?

    a. to explain why eating chilies is painful

    b. to show the effect of chilies on the mind

    c. to explain how chilies are good for you

DETAIL

3. How is capsaicin good for your health?

    a. It helps you breathe better.

    b. It makes you feel happier.

    c. It makes you feel hungrier.

DETAIL

4. Which of the following is NOT true about Anandita Dutta Tamuly?

    a. She is famous for eating Carolina Reaper chilies.

    b. She often eats chilies when she feels sick.

    c. She started eating chilies when she was a child.

⌃ **Many types of chilies turn from green to red as they grow.**

PARAPHRASING

5. In paragraph F, the phrase *I barely notice them* can be replaced with _____

    a. I usually don't eat hot chilies anymore.

    b. I feel the heat of the chilies even more.

    c. I almost don't feel the heat of the chilies.

MATCHING

B. Look back at the information in Reading B. Match each pepper (a–d) with the correct description.

a. Sweet Bell Pepper	b. Naga Jolokia	c. Tabasco	d. Carolina Reaper

1. _____ is the hottest chili in the world.

2. _____ is around 3 times the SHU of Thai Chili.

3. _____ is not as hot as jalapeño.

4. _____ is also known as "ghost pepper."

Pronoun Reference

Pronouns are words such as *he, she, it, they,* and *them,* and usually refer to a noun earlier in a passage. To understand a passage, it is important to know what each pronoun refers to.

Sara bought chilies. **She** *put* **them** *in my favorite curry.* **It** *was too hot to eat!*

REFERENCE **A.** In each sentence, draw an arrow from the pronoun in **bold** to the word it refers to, as in the examples above.

1. The jalapeño is a popular chili from Mexico. **It** takes its name from Jalapa, in Veracruz.

2. My brother and sister asked my mother not to put chilies in the food **she** made.

3. Chilies have been eaten in the Americas for thousands of years. Nowadays, **they** are popular all around the world.

4. Indians put chili peppers in many of their dishes. They often add **them** to curries.

⌃ **People in the Americas were eating chilies as early as 7500 B.C.**

REFERENCE **B.** Look back at Reading B. Find the following sentences in the passage. Write the word each pronoun in **bold** refers to.

1. Your mouth feels like **it**'s on fire. (paragraph A) it = _____

2. **It** helps you breathe better. (paragraph C) It = _____

3. She began eating chilies when **she** was a child. (paragraph F) she = _____

4. To be honest, I barely notice **them** now. (paragraph F) them = _____

CRITICAL THINKING Applying Ideas

▶ Work with a partner. Think of four famous spicy foods. List them below.

_____ _____ _____ _____

▶ Now rank the foods in your list from 1–4 (1 = the hottest).

COMPLETION   **A.** Complete the information using the words in the box.

| contains | dishes | health | painful | plants |

They may not look tasty, but some types of cactus ¹_____ can be eaten and are very good for your ²_____. In Mexico, *nopalitos*—young stems of the cactus—have been eaten for hundreds of years.

Eating cactus has recently become more popular outside of Mexico. There are many tasty ³_____ that use cactus stems. Here is one way to cook them.

- Clean and cut up the stems. Don't cut yourself on the sharp parts of the plant! That can be ⁴_____.

- Next, heat some oil in a pan and add the cactus. Then add some salt and cover the pan.

- The cactus ⁵_____ a strange liquid. Cook the cactus until all the liquid comes out and dries up. Then enjoy!

∧ **A man cuts and cleans cactus stems in a Mexican market.**

DEFINITIONS   **B.** Match each word in **red** with its definition.

1. **plant**   •   • a. healthy and strong
2. **hungry**   •   • b. needing food
3. **breathe**   •   • c. a living thing that usually grows in the ground
4. **fit**   •   • d. to take air in and out

COLLOCATIONS   **C.** The words in the box are often used with the adjective **painful**. Complete the sentences using the correct words.

| cut | lesson | memory |

1. Looking at the old photo brought back a painful _____.
2. The chef's knife slipped, so he got a painful _____ on his hand.
3. Failing my first exam was a painful _____. I'll study harder for the next one.

SCIENCE OF TASTE

∧ A tea buyer tastes a selection of teas.

BEFORE YOU WATCH

PREVIEWING **A.** Read the information. The words in **bold** appear in the video. Match each word with the type of food it describes.

1. **sweet** •   • a. potato chips
2. **salty** •   • b. candy
3. **sour** •   • c. dark chocolate
4. **bitter** •   • d. lime

PREVIEWING **B.** Work with a partner. List three more foods for each category in activity A.

_____

_____

_____

_____

GIST **A.** Watch the video. What senses do we use when we taste food? Note your answers below.

_____

_____

DETAILS **B.** Watch the video again. Complete the sentences with the words and phrases (a–d) in the box. Each option can be used more than once.

| a. more bitter | b. saltier | c. more sour | d. sweeter |

1. Red food tastes _____.   **4.** White food tastes _____.

2. Green food tastes _____.   **5.** Food on a round plate tastes _____.

3. Black food tastes _____.   **6.** Food on a square plate tastes _____.

CRITICAL THINKING Applying Ideas   Imagine you are the owner of a restaurant. You want to serve healthier food, but you still want it to taste good. What ideas from the video might help you do this? Note your ideas below. Then discuss with a partner.

_____

_____

_____

_____

VOCABULARY REVIEW

Do you remember the meanings of these words? Check (✓) the ones you know. Look back at the unit and review any words you're not sure of.

Reading A

☐ argue   ☐ athlete   ☐ exactly   ☐ record

☐ tradition*   ☐ unhealthy   ☐ various   ☐ work out

Reading B

☐ breathe   ☐ contain   ☐ dish   ☐ fit

☐ health   ☐ hungry   ☐ painful   ☐ plant

* Academic Word List

3

COOL
JOBS

An astronomer prepares for work at the Mount Wilson Observatory, United States.

3A

Nora Shawki achieved her lifelong **goal** of becoming an **archeologist**, but there were **challenges** along the way.

BEFORE YOU READ

DEFINITIONS **A.** Look at the photo and read the caption. Match each word in **bold** with its definition.

1. archeologist •   • a. something you hope to achieve
2. challenge •   • b. a difficult situation
3. goal •   • c. a person who finds and studies objects from the past

SKIMMING **B.** What challenges do you think Nora Shawki might have faced in her career? Discuss your ideas with a partner. Then skim the passage to see which of your ideas are mentioned.

DIGGING
FOR THE PAST

by Nora Shawki

A When I was in third grade, I watched a video that recreated the discovery of King Tutankhamen's tomb. I remember Howard Carter[1] peering through a narrow hole in the tomb with a candle. A workman asked what he could see: "Wonderful things!" Carter said. From that moment, I knew what I wanted to do with my life.

B Today, I'm **lucky** to work as an archeologist. I study the lives of people who lived in Egypt's Nile Delta. It's exciting work. Sometimes you find something that was buried three thousand years ago. Holding a piece of **history** is an **amazing** feeling.

C So I **decided** what I wanted to be at the age of nine, and I made it happen. Seems easy, right? Not quite! The road wasn't easy. I did my studies—university, then a PhD. But along the way I was told many things: I was too young, I wasn't qualified, I should **get married** and have kids. I also needed money, so I applied for six grants.[2] The first five replies I got said *no*. Six months later, the last reply came: This time it was *yes*. Finally, I could start my own excavation.[3]

D For anyone thinking about a **career**, I would say: Never give up. If you want to do something, keep trying. If people tell you *no*, use that—it will push you. At the beginning, it **hurts**. But the next *no* hurts a little less. It makes you stronger and actually helps you.

E Second, focus on your goals. And I stress *yours*. You don't have to **follow** other people. If they say something has never been done, make it happen. You may be the first to do it! There are always challenges, but you overcome them in the end.

---

1 **Howard Carter** was a British archeologist who became famous for discovering the tomb of Tutankhamen in 1922.

2 A **grant** is money given by a government or organization for a special project.

3 An **excavation** involves removing earth to search for very old objects buried in the ground.

A. Choose the best answer for each question.

GIST **1.** What could be another title for the reading?

    a. Following a Childhood Dream

    b. A Day in the Life of an Archeologist

    c. The Nile Delta's Hidden Treasures

PURPOSE **2.** What is the purpose of paragraph A?

    a. to explain the challenges Shawki faced at school

    b. to describe what was found inside Tutankhamen's tomb

    c. to explain how Shawki became interested in archeology

SEQUENCE **3.** Which of the following happened first?

    a. Shawki applied for a grant.

    b. Shawki went to university.

    c. Shawki decided to be an archeologist.

DETAIL **4.** Which of the following is NOT given as a challenge Shawki faced?

    a. Others didn't agree with her career choice.

    b. She needed to take care of her family.

    c. It was difficult to get money for excavations.

VOCABULARY **5.** In paragraph E, what does *stress* mean?

    a. a feeling you have when your life is difficult

    b. to make it clear that something is important

    c. to introduce a new idea or opinion

MATCHING HEADINGS **B.** Match each paragraph with a suitable heading.

    1. Paragraph B •   • a. Be the First

    2. Paragraph C •   • b. Stay Positive

    3. Paragraph D •   • c. A Dream Come True

    4. Paragraph E •   • d. Overcoming Challenges

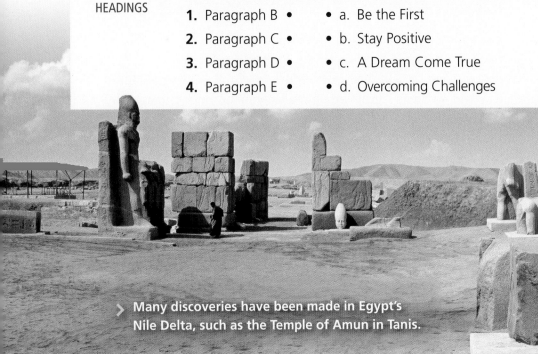

> **Many discoveries have been made in Egypt's Nile Delta, such as the Temple of Amun in Tanis.**

Dealing with New Vocabulary (1)—Using a Dictionary

When you look up a new word in a dictionary, there is often more than one definition. To find the correct definition, first identify its part of speech (e.g., noun, verb, adjective, adverb). Then look at the other words in the sentence to help you find the correct definition.

MATCHING **A.** Identify the part of speech of the word **past** in each sentence below. Then match each sentence to the correct definition.

1. Archeologists study the **past**. •   • a. (adj) previous
2. They drove **past** the museum. •   • b. (prep) after a certain time
3. I was away this **past** weekend. •   • c. (prep) beyond a certain place
4. It's 20 minutes **past** six. •   • d. (n) the time before now

COMPLETION **B.** Circle the part of speech for each underlined word. Then look up the word in a dictionary, and write down its definition.

1. I study the lives of people who lived in Egypt's Nile Delta. (paragraph B)

   part of speech: **noun / verb**

   definition: _____

2. I did my studies. (paragraph C)

   part of speech: **noun / verb**

   definition: _____

3. The first five replies I got said *no*. (paragraph C)

   part of speech: **noun / verb**

   definition: _____

4. Second, focus on your goals. (paragraph E)

   part of speech: **noun / verb**

   definition: _____

CRITICAL THINKING Evaluating Advice

▶ Rate each piece of career advice below 1–5 (5 = great advice, 1 = bad advice).

a. Don't worry about money. Choose a job you love.   _____

b. It's important to get a job at a big company.   _____

c. Don't listen to other people. Only your opinion matters.   _____

d. Qualifications aren't important if you have talent.   _____

e. The best way to be successful is to start your own business.   _____

f. Dream jobs rarely happen. Aim for something more realistic.   _____

▶ Compare your answers with a partner and explain your reasons.

COMPLETION **A.** Complete the information using the words in the box.

career	decide	follow	history	lucky

Do you love ¹_____? If so, there are some interesting ²_____ paths that you can ³_____. Some people work as archeologists or historians. Others might ⁴_____ to work as teachers, librarians, tour guides, or researchers.

Another interesting job is that of a "living historian." Living historians work as actors at historical sites. They wear traditional clothes and speak in the language from that time. Visitors who are ⁵_____ enough to speak to a living historian can ask them questions about life at that time.

∧ **A living historian wears 18th-century clothing in Virginia, United States.**

DEFINITIONS **B.** Choose the correct word or phrase to complete each sentence below.

1. If something **hurts** you badly, you may *cry / smile*.
2. If something is **amazing**, it is very *bad or boring / good or surprising*.
3. When you **get married**, you have a *husband or wife / son or daughter*.

COLLOCATIONS **C.** The adjectives below can be used with the verb **get**. Complete the sentences using the words in the diagram.

1. It's easy to get _____ in the dark.
2. We need to get _____ to leave. Class starts in 10 minutes.
3. I get _____ when I work all day without a break.
4. If I feel like I'm getting _____, I take some deep breaths and count to 10.

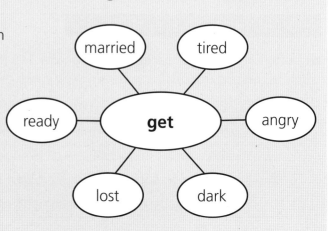

BEFORE YOU READ

A. Look at the photo and read the caption. Then discuss these questions with a partner.

    1. What kinds of things do you usually take photos of?

    2. Do you think a photographer's job is easy?

B. Skim the interview on pages 42–43. Then write each interview question (a–d) above its answer in the passage.

    a. I want to be a photographer. Do you have any advice for me?

    b. What kind of photographers is *National Geographic* looking for?

    c. Is it difficult to get a job as a photographer today?

    d. How did you become a *National Geographic* photographer?

National Geographic photographer Joel Sartore photographs an Adélie penguin chick in Antarctica.

∧ Joel Sartore prepares to take a photo
of a frill-necked lizard.

GETTING THE SHOT

An interview with Joel Sartore

A   *Joel Sartore is a writer, teacher, and photographer. His words—and beautiful images—show his love of photography and of the natural world. He was* National Geographic's *2018 Explorer of the Year.*

Question 1: _____

B   My first job was for a newspaper. After a few years there, I met a *National Geographic* photographer. He liked my photos and said I should send some to the magazine. So I did. That led to a one-day job. And that led to a nine-day job, and so on.

Question 2: _____

C   To get into *National Geographic*, you have to give them something they don't have. It's not **enough** just to be a great photographer. You also have to be a scientist, for example, or be able to dive under sea ice, or **spend** maybe **several** days in a tree.

Question 3: _____

D   It's now more difficult to work for magazines. Technology makes it easy to take good pictures, which means there are more photos and photographers. Also, the Web is full of photos from all around the world that are **free**, or **cost** very little. These photos are often good enough to be put in books and magazines that once **paid** for photographers and their photos.

Question 4: _____

E   Advice? Well, work hard. Be passionate[1] about every **project** you work on. Take lots of pictures in different **situations**. Look at others' photos thoughtfully and learn from them. And be curious[2] about life. There's something to photograph everywhere.

F   But be a photographer for the right reasons. If you do it for the money, you probably won't really be happy. Do you want to make the world a better place, or make people see things in a different way? If so, you'll enjoy the work much more.

---

1 A **passionate** person has very strong feelings about something.

2 If you are **curious** about something, you want to know more about it.

A. Choose the best answer for each question.

VOCABULARY

1. In the title "Getting the Shot," what does the word *shot* mean?

a. job   b. photo   c. magazine

DETAIL

2. Which of the following sentences about Joel Sartore is NOT true?

a. His first job was with *National Geographic*.
b. He once worked for a newspaper.
c. He is also a writer.

MAIN IDEA

3. What was Sartore's main point in his answer to Question 3?

a. Photographers need to use more technology.
b. Putting your photos online can lead to other jobs.
c. It's not easy to get paid work as a photographer these days.

PARAPHRASING

4. In paragraph E, the sentence *There's something to photograph everywhere* is closest in meaning to _____

a. With new technology, anyone can be a photographer.
b. Take more photos than you think you will need.
c. You can find interesting things in many different places.

MAIN IDEA

5. What is the main idea of paragraph F?

a. You should try to see people in different ways.
b. If you work hard, you can make money as a photographer.
c. You should ask yourself why you want to be a photographer.

⌃ **In 2015, some of Sartore's photos were projected onto the Empire State Building, New York.**

PRONOUN REFERENCE

Review this reading skill in Unit 2B

B. Look back at Reading B. What does each pronoun refer to? Circle the correct option.

1. there (paragraph B)

a. at the newspaper   b. at the magazine

2. some (paragraph B)

a. Joel Sartore's photos   b. *National Geographic*'s photos

3. them (paragraph E)

a. different situations   b. other people's photos

4. it (paragraph F)

a. become a photographer   b. take a photograph

Understanding Suffixes

A suffix is one or more letters that can be added to the end of a word to make a new word. The suffix usually changes the word to a different form, such as from a noun to an adjective. Knowing some of the most common suffixes can help you guess the meaning of unfamiliar words as you read. Here are some examples with their usual meanings.

Suffix	Examples
-er / -or / -ist = person who does	*painter, actor, guitarist*
-ful / -fully = full of	*colorful, playful, playfully*
-al = relating to	*musical, natural*

SCANNING **A.** Look back at the first paragraph of Reading B. Find and circle four words with the suffix *-er*.

COMPLETION **B.** In each sentence from Reading B below, underline any words that contain a suffix from the box above. Then write a simple definition of each one.

1. His words—and beautiful images—show his love of photography and the natural world.

_____

_____

2. To get into *National Geographic*, you have to give them something they don't have.

_____

3. Look at others' photos thoughtfully and learn from them.

_____

DEFINITIONS **C.** Look back at Reading A, "Digging for the Past." Find and write a word that contains each suffix below. Then write a sentence with each word.

1. *-ful* (paragraph A) _____   **2.** *-ist* (paragraph B) _____

_____

_____

CRITICAL THINKING Personalizing

▶ Write three questions you would like to ask Joel Sartore.

1. _____ ?

2. _____ ?

3. _____ ?

▶ Compare with a partner. How do you think Sartore would answer your questions?

COMPLETION **A.** Complete the information using the words in the box.

enough	project	several	situation	spent

Stories Behind the Shots

Joel Sartore takes studio photos of animals as part of a ¹_____ called the Photo Ark. The aim is to raise awareness of endangered species. Sartore usually takes ²_____ images of the same animal, but things don't always go according to plan.

Joel Sartore took this photo of an ocelot at a zoo in the United States. He ³_____ a lot of time with the animal, but getting the shot was not easy. "They hardly ever hold still," says Sartore. "So I really had to act quickly." Many animals will stand still only long ⁴_____ to get food. After they eat, the photo shoot is over.

Behind this image is another great story. At an aquarium, Sartore came across a very angry frog. While he tried to take a photo of it, it tried to bite him. He never thought he would be in a ⁵_____ where he was afraid of a frog! "First time for everything," says Sartore.

DEFINITIONS **B.** Match the two parts of each definition.

1. When you **pay** for something, •   • a. it is expensive.
2. If something **costs** a lot of money, •   • b. you don't need to give money for it.
3. If something is **free**, •   • c. you give money for it.

WORD FORMS **C.** The verbs **pay**, **cost**, and **spend** have irregular past tense forms. Write the past tense form of each verb in the chart below. Then complete the sentences using the correct words.

pay → _____   cost → _____   spend → _____

1. I _____ in cash for my new camera.
2. It doesn't _____ much to take a photography class.
3. My parents _____ a lot of money on their new car.

> At Canine Assistants, dogs learn to be more than just pets.

RIGHT DOG FOR THE JOB

BEFORE YOU WATCH

PREVIEWING **A.** Read the information. The words in **bold** appear in the video. Match the correct form of each word with its definition.

Since 1991, Canine Assistants has **trained** over 1,500 dogs. These "super-dogs" learn more than just tricks. Once their **training** is complete, the dogs will be given to people who need help in their daily lives. These dogs have an important job to do and many things to learn. It is the animal **trainers'** job to teach them to do it.

1. _____ (v) to teach how to do a job

2. _____ (n) someone who teaches others how to do a job

3. _____ (n) the process of learning how to do a job

PREDICTING **B.** What do you think the dogs in the video learn to do? Check (✓) your ideas from the skills below.

☐ pick up things   ☐ call the police   ☐ turn lights on

☐ run in a race   ☐ open/close doors   ☐ be comfortable with people

☐ find help   ☐ drive a car   ☐ swim

☐ buy groceries   ☐ use a phone   ☐ get along with other animals

GIST **A.** Watch the video. Check your ideas in Before You Watch B.

DETAILS **B.** Watch the video again. Complete the sentences using the phrases in the box. One is extra.

a. are given food	b. are taken outside the camp	c. train in the puppy room
d. want to help their owners	e. find everything frightening	f. push a large button

1. During training, the dogs _____ when they do something right.

2. According to Jennifer Arnold, it's important that the dogs _____.

3. Before they are 16 weeks old, the dogs _____.

4. At around 8 weeks old, the dogs _____.

5. They _____ to show there is nothing to be afraid of.

CRITICAL THINKING Synthesizing Information Look at the jobs in the box below. Consider what you've learned in this unit about each one. Which job would you most like to have? Note your ideas and explain your reasons to a partner.

archeologist	**living historian**	**wildlife photographer**	**dog trainer**

VOCABULARY REVIEW

Do you remember the meanings of these words? Check (✓) the ones you know. Look back at the unit and review any words you're not sure of.

Reading A

☐ amazing   ☐ career   ☐ decide   ☐ follow

☐ get married   ☐ history   ☐ hurt   ☐ lucky

Reading B

☐ cost   ☐ enough   ☐ free   ☐ pay

☐ project*   ☐ several   ☐ situation   ☐ spend

*Academic Word List

4

SHIPWRECKS

A diver investigates the wreck of a sailing boat off the coast of Egypt.

DEFINITIONS **A.** Look at the picture and read the timeline. Check each word in **bold** in a dictionary.

> Review this reading skill in Unit 3A

PREVIEWING **B.** Look at the picture and timeline again. Answer the questions.

1. What caused the *Titanic* to sink?

2. Why did so many people die?

3. When did explorers find the *Titanic* again? How did they study it?

SCANNING **C.** Read the first sentence of each paragraph of the reading passage on the next two pages. How many times did Robert Ballard explore the *Titanic*? Read the whole passage to check your answer.

> Called the "Ship of Dreams," the *Titanic* was the biggest passenger ship of its time.

April 10, 1912
The *Titanic* leaves England for New York.

April 14, 11:40 p.m.
The *Titanic* hits an **iceberg**.

April 15, 12:00–2:20 a.m.
Water begins to fill the ship's lower levels. **Passengers,** mostly women and children, get into small **lifeboats**. But there aren't enough.

I'VE FOUND THE TITANIC!

A   As a boy, Robert Ballard liked to read about shipwrecks. He read a lot about the *Titanic*. "My lifelong dream was to find this great ship," he says.

B   On August 31, 1985, Ballard's dream came true. He found the wreck of the *Titanic*. The ship was in two main parts, lying four kilometers under the sea. Using video cameras and an undersea robot,[1] Ballard looked around the ship. He found many items that told the sad story of the *Titanic*'s end. For example, he found a child's shoes, a reminder[2] of the many deaths that happened that night in 1912.

---

1   A **robot** is a machine controlled by a computer.
2   A **reminder** of something makes you remember it.

April 15, 2:20 a.m.
The ship breaks into two and sinks;
1,514 people die that night.

August 31, 1985 The **shipwreck**
of the *Titanic* is found after 73 years.
Explorers use deep-sea **submarines**
to study it.

C In 1986, Ballard visited the *Titanic* again. This time, he **reached** the ship in a small submarine. A deep-sea robot took photos inside the ship. When other people saw the photos, they wanted to visit the ship, too.

D When Ballard **returned** in 2004, he found the *Titanic* in very bad **condition**. Other explorers had taken away about 6,000 items, like clothes, dishes, and shoes. Some even took pieces of the ship. They think these things should be moved to a safer place, but Ballard doesn't **agree**.

E Ballard believes that taking things from the *Titanic* is wrong. **Instead**, he wants to put lights and cameras on and around the shipwreck. This way, people can see the great ship and remember what happened to it. "As long as she needs protection,"[3] says Ballard, "the *Titanic* will always be part of my life."

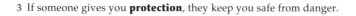

3 If someone gives you **protection**, they keep you safe from danger.

∧ **Deep-sea explorer Robert Ballard**

‹ **Lights from a submarine show the inside of a first-class cabin on the wreck of the *Titanic*.**

A. Choose the best answer for each question.

GIST

1. What is the reading mainly about?

    a. how visitors to the *Titanic* leave it in bad condition

    b. Robert Ballard's hopes that more people will visit the *Titanic*

    c. how Robert Ballard found the *Titanic* and wants to keep it safe

DETAIL

2. The first time he explored the *Titanic*, Ballard did NOT _____.

    a. visit the shipwreck in a submarine

    b. find a child's shoes in the shipwreck

    c. use a robot to look around the shipwreck

DETAIL

3. According to the passage, what did people see that made them want to visit the *Titanic*?

    a. the submarine Ballard used

    b. photos from inside the ship

    c. items that were taken from the ship

△ The *Titanic* just before its first and final trip in 1912

REFERENCE

4. In paragraph D, who does *They* refer to?

    a. Robert Ballard and his team

    b. other visitors to the *Titanic* shipwreck

    c. people from the *Titanic* who are still alive

INFERENCE

5. Which statement would Ballard probably agree with?

    a. People should not remove anything from the *Titanic*.

    b. Lights and cameras will hurt the remains of the *Titanic*.

    c. The *Titanic* wreck should be moved out of the water completely.

SUMMARIZING

B. Complete the summary. Choose the correct options (a–f).

a. a child's shoes	b. an undersea robot	c. a small submarine
d. lights and cameras	e. thousands of items	f. very bad condition

In 1985, Robert Ballard found the wreck of the *Titanic*. He used ¹_____ to look around the ship. He found many items left by passengers such as ²_____. In 1986, Ballard visited the wreck again. This time, he reached it in ³_____. When he returned again in 2004, he found the *Titanic* in ⁴_____. Other explorers had removed ⁵_____. Ballard wants to protect the ship by putting ⁶_____ around it.

Identifying a Paragraph's Main Idea

Most paragraphs have one main idea. To determine the main idea of a paragraph, ask yourself, "What point is the author trying to make?" The first and last sentences of a paragraph, as well as its heading (if it has one), can also give you clues about the main idea.

IDENTIFYING
MAIN IDEAS

A. **What is the main idea of the text below? Circle the correct option.**

a. The *Carpathia* took over three hours to get to the *Titanic*.

b. The *Carpathia* answered the *Titanic*'s call and helped save lives.

c. The *Carpathia* was too far away to help stop the *Titanic* from sinking.

On April 15, 1912, at 12:20 a.m., the British ship *Carpathia* got a message from the *Titanic*. The "Ship of Dreams" was sinking. The *Carpathia* was 93 kilometers away. It traveled at top speed to where the *Titanic* was, even though there were dangerous icebergs in the ocean. It arrived at 3:30 a.m., over an hour after the *Titanic* sank. Still, the *Carpathia* was able to pick up 711 people. The ship then went to New York, arriving there on April 18.

IDENTIFYING
MAIN IDEAS

B. **Look back at Reading A. What is the main idea of each paragraph? Circle the correct options.**

Paragraph A: a. Ballard read a lot about the *Titanic*.

b. Ballard's dream was to find the *Titanic*.

Paragraph B: a. Ballard found items like a child's shoes.

b. Ballard finally found the shipwreck he was looking for.

Paragraph C: a. Ballard reached the ship in a small submarine.

b. Ballard returned and took photos of the ship.

Paragraph D: a. Some explorers had found shoes at the wreck.

b. The *Titanic* was in bad condition when Ballard returned.

Paragraph E: a. Ballard wants to protect the *Titanic*.

b. Ballard wants to put lights and cameras around the ship.

CRITICAL THINKING Evaluating Arguments

▶ The reading passage states that Robert Ballard "believes that taking things from the *Titanic* is wrong." Why do you think he feels this way?

▶ Complete the chart below with arguments for and against taking items from the *Titanic*. Share your ideas with a partner. Do you agree with Robert Ballard?

Arguments for taking items	Arguments against taking items

COMPLETION   **A.** Complete the information using the words in the box. One word is extra.

conditions   deaths   items   reach   returned

Why were there so many ¹_____ on the night the *Titanic* sank? One reason was the freezing ²_____. Experts believe most people who fell into the water died from the cold in under 15 minutes. However, the main reason was that there were not enough lifeboats. There were 2,223 people on the ship, but lifeboats for only 1,186 people. Also, many people could not ³_____ the boats before the ship sank. In the end, only 705 people ⁴_____ safely to land.

⌃ **At first, most people could not believe the news of the *Titanic*'s sinking.**

COMPLETION   **B.** Complete the sentences. Choose the correct words.

1. If people **agree**, they have _____ about a subject.
   a. the same idea   b. different ideas

2. If you drink tea **instead** of coffee, you drink _____.
   a. tea   b. both tea and coffee

3. An example of an **item** of clothing is _____.
   a. warmth   b. a jacket

4. A lifelong **dream** is something you have _____ all your life.
   a. wanted to do   b. tried to stop doing

WORD USAGE   **C.** The verb **agree** can be followed by the prepositions *with*, *to*, and *on*.

You **agree with** a person (e.g., *I don't agree with you*).

You **agree to** do something (e.g., *I agreed to help my friend*).

You **agree on** something (e.g., *Everyone agreed on the cause of the problem*).

Complete the sentences. Circle the correct prepositions.

1. We couldn't agree *with / to / on* where to go for lunch.

2. I don't often agree *with / to / on* my parents.

3. Thanks for agreeing *with / to / on* work this weekend.

BEFORE YOU READ

SKIMMING FOR
MAIN IDEAS

Review this
reading skill
in Unit 4A

A. Skim the first three paragraphs of the reading. Match each paragraph to its main idea.

1. Paragraph A •   • a. There was a problem during the expedition.

2. Paragraph B •   • b. The team came up with a plan.

3. Paragraph C •   • c. Corey Jaskolski was part of a team that explored the *Titanic*.

SKIMMING FOR
MAIN IDEAS

B. Skim the rest of the reading. Was the team's plan a success? Read the passage to check your ideas.

> Corey Jaskolski and two crewmembers reached the wreck of the *Titanic* in a small submarine.

MY DESCENT
TO THE TITANIC

by Corey Jaskolski

A In 2001, I was part of an expedition[1] to explore the *Titanic*. Our team used two small deep-sea robots, one blue and one green. My job was to make sure the robots' **batteries** worked well.

∧ **Corey Jaskolski**

B Three days into the expedition, the green robot got stuck inside the *Titanic*. Even worse, one of its batteries was damaged. That was dangerous, as the battery could explode. It could harm the robot and the ship. We had to find a way to get it out.

C In the middle of the ocean, though, there are no stores to buy supplies. So, we had an idea. We took a coat hanger[2] and put it inside the blue robot. The **plan** was to use the hanger's hook[3] to **pull** out the green robot.

D Two crew members and I got ready to go down in a three-man submarine. A crane lifted us and placed us in the water. Then we started to sink—12,500 feet to the ocean bottom. If anything went wrong, we were **totally** on our own.

E At about 9,000 feet, a crewmate accidentally touched some wires. Suddenly, all the sub's lights went out. We were in complete darkness. It was terrifying, but the **pilot** was able to **fix** it, and we **carried on**.

F Finally, we reached the *Titanic*'s wreckage. First, we could just see pieces of **metal**. Then we started to see suitcases and shoes. Over a thousand people fell here, but their bodies disappeared long ago.

G For about 12 hours, we tried to pull the robot out with the coat hanger. Finally, we got it and brought it to the surface. There was no way we were going to leave it behind. That little robot was part of our team.

---

1 An **expedition** is a trip organized for a specific purpose.
2 A **coat hanger** is an object used to hang clothes in closets.
3 A **hook** is a curved piece of metal used to attach one thing to another.

A. Choose the best answer for each question.

GIST

1. What was Jaskolski's main job?

a. to build the robots for the mission
b. to drive the robots through the wreck of the *Titanic*
c. to make sure the robots' batteries didn't stop working

MAIN IDEA

2. What was the problem with the robot?

a. It exploded and damaged the ship.
b. It was trapped inside the wreck.
c. The team lost it in the dark water.

PARAPHRASING

3. Which sentence is closest in meaning to *we were totally on our own*?

a. We had to control the robots ourselves.
b. It was a very lonely feeling in the submarine.
c. There was nobody who could help us.

DETAIL

4. What caused the problem described in paragraph E?

a. the pilot
b. a robot
c. a crewmate

VOCABULARY

5. In paragraph F, what does *fell* mean?

a. died
b. dropped
c. tripped

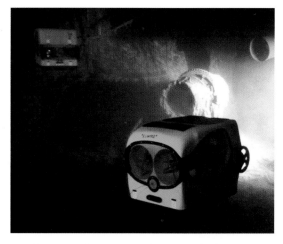

∧ **The two deep-sea robots Jaskolski used to study the *Titanic* wreck**

SUMMARIZING

B. Complete the sentences with the options (a–c) in the box. Each option can be used more than once.

a. the blue robot	b. the green robot	c. the submarine

1. There was a problem with the batteries in _____.

2. A hook was attached to _____.

3. A crane was used to put _____ into the water

4. There was a problem with _____ when somebody touched some wires.

5. The crew eventually used _____ to pull out _____.

Recognizing Compound Subjects and Objects

A sentence can have a single subject or a compound subject. A compound subject is a subject that contains two or more nouns. Sentences can also contain compound objects. Look at the examples below.

Compound subject: (_Ballard_ and _his team_) _found the_ Titanic _in 1985._

Compound object: _Ballard used_ (_cameras_ and _a robot_) _to look at the ship._

ANALYZING **A.** Find and circle examples of compound subjects and objects in the passage below. In each example, underline the different subjects or objects.

On July 17, 1956, the _Andrea Doria_ left Italy for New York. The ship was carrying over 1,700 passengers and crew members. A week later, the _Stockholm_ left New York for Sweden. That night, the _Andrea Doria_ and _Stockholm_ crossed paths with tragic results. Just after 11:00 p.m., the _Stockholm_ smashed into the side of the _Andrea Doria_. The _Andrea Doria_ began to sink slowly. The _Stockholm_ helped with the rescue of the passengers, but there would be 52 deaths that night. Were darkness and bad weather the cause of the accident? It remains a mystery to this day.

^ The _Andrea Doria_ sank shortly after this photo was taken.

SCANNING **B.** Find examples of compound subjects and objects in Reading B. Note them below.

1. Paragraph B: compound object: _____ and _____

2. Paragraph D: compound subject: _____ and _____

3. Paragraph F: compound object: _____ and _____

CRITICAL THINKING Evaluating Ideas   What are the advantages of sending robots to look at shipwrecks? What are the advantages of sending humans in submarines? Note some ideas in the chart below. Then discuss with a partner.

Advantages of Robots	Advantages of Humans

DEFINITIONS **A.** Read the information. Then complete the definitions using the correct form of the words in **red**.

Up to now, **battery**-powered robots have mostly explored the *Titanic*, along with a few lucky **pilots** and crew members in deep-sea submarines. For the average person, a visit to the famous wreck has only been a dream. That could change, as several companies **plan** to take visitors there in the future. The cost? Over $100,000.

Not everyone thinks these trips are a good idea, but if you decide to go, you may want to act fast. Harmful bacteria is eating away at the wreck. Some people believe that the ship could **totally** disappear in a few decades.

1. A _____ is someone who flies a plane or steers a ship.

2. A _____ is a small device that provides power for electrical items.

3. When you _____ something, you decide in detail what to do.

4. When you say _____, it means *completely* or *wholly*.

COMPLETION **B.** Complete each sentence with a word from the box.

carry on	fix	metal	pull

1. The *Titanic* was made mainly of _____. The wrecks of wooden ships do not last as long.

2. Robert Ballard says he will _____ working to protect the wreck of the *Titanic* for as long as necessary.

3. The arm of the robot sub is not working properly. Someone needs to come and _____ it before it can be used again.

4. After we finished our dive, we asked the crew to _____ us and our equipment out of the water.

WORD WEB **C.** There are many words that have the same meaning as **totally**. Complete the diagram below. Use a dictionary to help.

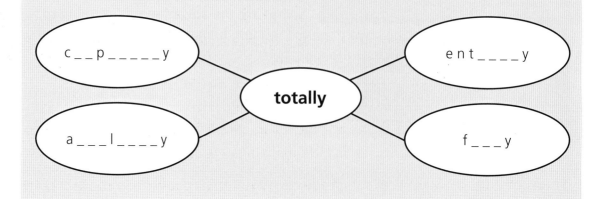

c _ _ p _ _ _ _ _ y

e n t _ _ _ _ _ y

totally

a _ _ _ l _ _ _ _ y

f _ _ _ y

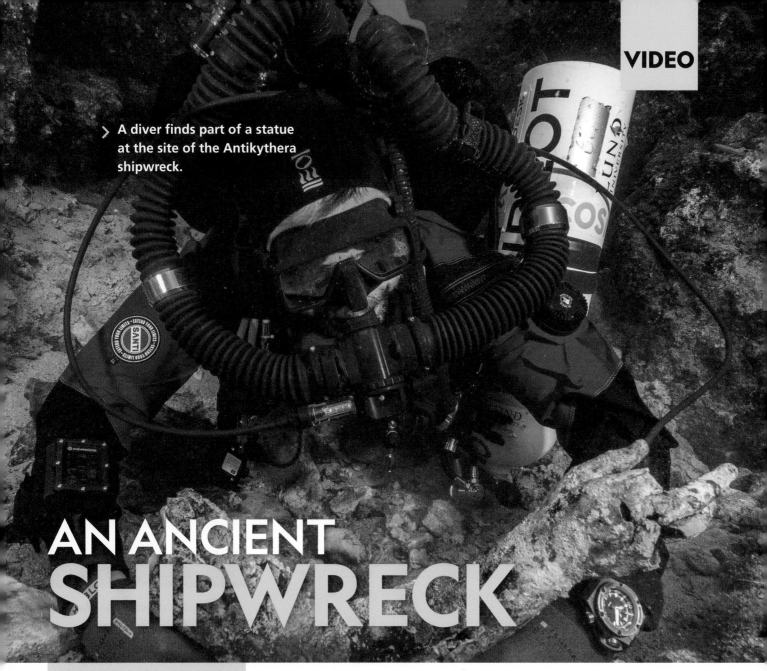

> A diver finds part of a statue at the site of the Antikythera shipwreck.

AN ANCIENT SHIPWRECK

BEFORE YOU WATCH

PREVIEWING

A. Read the information. The words in **bold** appear in the video. Match each word with its definition.

On the **seabed** near the Greek island of Antikythera, an **ancient** shipwreck can be found. Experts believe that the ship likely sank around 2,000 years ago on its way to Rome. Since the wreck was discovered, many archeologists have visited the site. Some of the objects found include pieces of **statues** and other strange items.

1. _____ (adj) very old

2. _____ (n) models of people made from stone or metal

3. _____ (n) the bottom of the ocean

DISCUSSION

B. What other kinds of objects do you think could be found in a 2,000-year-old shipwreck? Discuss with a partner.

GIST **A.** Watch the video. Which of the following is the best summary? Circle the correct option.

    a. A strange statue found at the Antikythera shipwreck has been a mystery for over a hundred years.

    b. Though the Antikythera shipwreck was first found over one hundred years ago, interesting discoveries continue to be made.

MATCHING **B.** Match each item in the box (a–c) with a description (1–5). Each item can be used more than once.

a. the Antikythera mechanism	b. the metal arm	c. the metal disk

1. ____ and ____ were discovered in 2017.

2. ____ was discovered in 1900.

3. ____ was used to study the stars.

4. No one knows what ____ was used for.

5. ____ is sometimes called an "ancient computer."

CRITICAL THINKING Justifying Ideas

▶ What do you think the metal disk discovered in the Antikythera shipwreck was? Look at the possibilities in the box below. Add two of your own ideas.

a coin	a medal	a shield
a toy	_____	_____

∧ **An artist's drawing of the disk found at the shipwreck**

▶ Discuss with a partner. Use information from the video to support your ideas.

VOCABULARY REVIEW

Do you remember the meanings of these words? Check (✓) the ones you know. Look back at the unit and review any words you're not sure of.

Reading A

☐ agree   ☐ condition   ☐ death   ☐ dream

☐ instead   ☐ item*   ☐ reach   ☐ return

Reading B

☐ battery   ☐ carry on   ☐ fix   ☐ metal

☐ pilot   ☐ plan   ☐ pull   ☐ totally

*Academic Word List

SCIENCE INVESTIGATORS

WARM UP

Discuss these questions with a partner.

1. What is the investigator in the photo doing?

2. In what other ways can science help to solve crimes?

An investigator at an FBI training facility learns how lasers can be used to work out the flight path of bullets.

BEFORE YOU READ

PREVIEWING   **A.** Look at the title and the photos. What do you think a "disease detective" does? Discuss your ideas with a partner.

SKIMMING   **B.** Skim the reading and check your ideas in activity A.

THE DISEASE DETECTIVE

A Six children were in the hospital. They were very sick, but the doctors didn't know what to do. They called Dr. Richard Besser, an **expert** on strange **illnesses**.

Finding a Cause

B First, Dr. Besser needed to find the cause of the illness. He looked for germs[1] in the children's bodies. In every child, Dr. Besser found the same type of the bacteria *E. coli*. He then looked at the bacteria's DNA.[2] It showed him that this type of *E. coli* was **dangerous**.

C Dr. Besser knew *E. coli* could move from animals to humans. Had the children **touched** animals that carried the bacteria? Besser found other *E. coli* cases in the area where the children lived. But it wasn't enough.

D Besser then made a **list** of what the sick children had eaten. They had all eaten cheese, apple juice, and fish. He then made a list of what healthy children in the area had eaten. They had eaten the cheese and fish, but not the apple juice.

Case Closed

E Besser went to where the apple juice was made. He saw animals around the apple trees. He also saw the workers using **dirty** apples that had fallen on the **ground**. More importantly, he saw that the apples were not washed before the juice was made, and that the juice was not heated. Doing these things would **kill** the bacteria. Besser then knew it was the apple juice that made the children sick.

F Besser's *E. coli* case had a happy ending. The children got better. And what Besser learned that day now helps keep others safe.

---

1 A **germ** is a very small living thing that can cause disease.
2 **DNA** is a chemical that contains information about a living thing's characteristics.

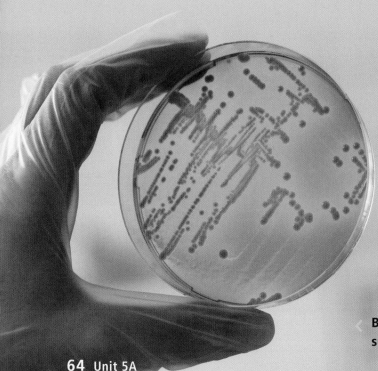

Bacteria are very small living things. Some bacteria, such as *E. coli*, can be dangerous to humans.

A. Choose the best answer for each question.

GIST

1. Another title for this passage could be _____.

a. Good vs. Bad Bacteria
b. Looking for Answers
c. A Death at the Hospital

SEQUENCE

2. Which of these things happened first?

a. Dr. Besser found out the illness was caused by *E. coli*.
b. Dr. Besser made a list of what the sick children ate.
c. Dr. Besser went to where the apple juice was made.

DETAIL

3. Which of the following is NOT true about *E. coli*?

a. It contains DNA.
b. It can make people sick.
c. There is only one type.

CAUSE AND EFFECT

4. What made the children sick?

a. old fish
b. dirty apples
c. smelly cheese

INFERENCE

5. What advice would Dr. Besser probably agree with?

a. Never drink apple juice from a supermarket. You should make it yourself.
b. Stay away from animals that live near trees. They will make you sick.
c. Don't eat fruit straight from the ground. Wash the fruit before you eat it.

▲ **Dr. Richard Besser is an expert on illnesses that move and kill quickly.**

SUMMARIZING

B. Complete the sentences. Use one to three words from the passage for each answer.

1. Dr. Besser knew the *E. coli* was dangerous after he looked at the bacteria's _____.

2. *E. coli* can be passed from _____.

3. The healthy children in the area had not drunk any _____.

4. There was bacteria in the juice because the apples were not _____ and the juice was not _____.

Identifying the Purpose of a Paragraph

Identifying a paragraph's purpose (or purposes) helps you understand the organization of a passage. The first line of a paragraph and its heading (if it has one) can give you clues about its purpose. These purposes can include:

- to introduce a topic
- to give an example
- to give data and statistics
- to give a conclusion

- to ask (or answer) a question
- to describe a problem
- to list a sequence of actions
- to describe a solution

IDENTIFYING PURPOSE

A. Look back at Reading A. Choose the main purpose of each paragraph.

1. Paragraph A
   a. to describe a problem
   b. to give an example

2. Paragraph D
   a. to list a sequence of actions
   b. to answer a question

3. Paragraph E
   a. to introduce a topic
   b. to answer a question

4. Paragraph F
   a. to give data and statistics
   b. to give a conclusion

IDENTIFYING PURPOSE

B. Look back at Unit 4, Reading B. Note the purpose of each paragraph below.

1. Paragraph A: _____
2. Paragraph B: _____
3. Paragraph C: _____
4. Paragraph D: _____
5. Paragraph G: _____

CRITICAL THINKING Applying Ideas

▶ Look back at paragraph E in Reading A. Write three rules that the apple juice factory should follow to make sure an *E. coli* case does not happen again.

_____
_____
_____

▶ Compare your ideas with a partner. Explain your reasons.

VOCABULARY PRACTICE

COMPLETION **A.** Complete the information using the words in the box.

dangerous	expert	illness	kill	touch

To most people, a bee sting is painful but not really

¹_____. However, for some, a little bee sting can

²_____. In fact, every year, there are many people who

die from bee stings. But scientists are learning that bee stings

can also be used to help people. Dr. Chris Kleronomos is a(n)

³_____ on natural medicines. He is trying to help a young

man named Erick. Erick has a(n) ⁴_____ that causes his muscles to hurt. He

experiences pain when people ⁵_____ him. Dr. Kleronomos uses the bee's

poison to take away Erick's pain. It may sound strange, but for people like Erick, it

seems to be working.

DEFINITIONS **B.** Complete the sentences. Circle the correct words.

1. If something is **dirty**, it is not *cheap / clean*.

2. A **list** usually has *just one thing / many things* on it.

3. If you see something on the **ground**, you are probably looking *down / up*.

4. An **expert** on a subject knows *a lot / very little* about it.

WORD FORMS **C.** The suffix *-ous* can be added to some nouns to make adjectives
(e.g., danger → **dangerous**). Complete the chart below.

Nouns		Adjective
danger	→	**dangerous**
_____	→	adventurous
fame	→	_____
_____	→	mysterious

Now complete the sentences using the correct form of the words above.

1. My road trip through New Zealand was a real _____.

2. The doctor had no idea about the cause of the illness. It was a(n) _____.

3. If you're _____, many people will recognize you.

BEFORE YOU READ

DEFINITIONS **A.** Look at the photo and caption. Complete the definitions using the correct form of the words in **bold**.

1. A _____ is a person who takes things they do not own.
2. A _____ is a piece of information that helps solve a crime.
3. A _____ is made when you touch something with your hands.

SCANNING **B.** Quickly scan the reading passage. Underline all the clues the crime scene investigator finds.

< Crime scene investigators look for many different types of **clues**, such as objects or **fingerprints** left by a **thief**.

AT THE SCENE OF A **CRIME**

A It's 5:30 a.m., and your phone rings. A police officer says someone broke into[1] a store and took some expensive items. They need you right away. It is your job to study the whole scene for clues that will help **catch** the thief. You are a crime scene investigator, and the game is on.

B Outside the store, you see a broken window, but there is no glass on the street. There are shoeprints, and marks made by a **vehicle**'s tires.[2] You look at the shoeprints. They're large, so you're likely looking for a man. You photograph the shoe's pattern. This can tell you the type of shoe. You then measure the **space** between the shoeprints. You now know how long the person's **steps** were. This gives you an idea of how tall the thief was.

C As you follow the shoeprints over to the tire marks, the spaces between the steps get bigger. They lead to the passenger's side of the vehicle. Now you know the thief probably didn't work **alone**. You photograph the tire marks. They can help you find out the type of vehicle and the **direction** it went.

D The most important clues will come from a person's body. You find some fingerprints near the broken window. Using a computer, you can **compare** these prints against millions of others. You also find a hair. You keep it, because you know hair contains a person's DNA. You can compare this with other people's DNA, too. If you find a match for the fingerprint or the DNA, you will know who was in the store.

E Will you find the thief? You now have a lot of information, so it's **possible**. For a crime scene investigator, it's all in a day's work.

---

1 If someone **breaks into** a place, they go inside even though they are not allowed to be there.

2 A **tire** is the outside of a car wheel. It is usually black and made of rubber.

A. Choose the best answer for each question.

GIST

1. What is the reading mainly about?

    a. how an investigator used clues to find a famous thief

    b. what a crime scene investigator looks for at a crime scene

    c. how thieves are using new technology to break into places

VOCABULARY

2. In paragraph B, what can the word *likely* be replaced with?

    a. carefully

    b. probably

    c. comfortably

REFERENCE

3. In the last sentence of paragraph B, what does *This* refer to?

    a. the size of the thief's shoes

    b. the distance between the thief's shoeprints

    c. the pattern on the bottom of the thief's shoes

⌃ **A crime scene investigator takes a photo of a shoeprint.**

DETAIL

4. Which of the following is NOT mentioned as something the investigator can learn from the tire marks?

    a. the direction the thief went

    b. how heavy the thief's car was

    c. the type of car the thief used

DETAIL

5. What are the most important clues that the investigator finds?

    a. fingerprints and a hair

    b. shoeprints and tire marks

    c. an item of clothing

EVALUATING STATEMENTS

B. Are the following statements true or false, or is the information not given in the passage? Circle T (true), F (false), or NG (not given).

1. The thief took nothing from the store.	**T**	**F**	**NG**
2. There were shoeprints outside the store.	**T**	**F**	**NG**
3. The tire marks were made by an expensive vehicle.	**T**	**F**	**NG**
4. The investigator collected DNA from the scene.	**T**	**F**	**NG**
5. Someone heard the noise from the crime.	**T**	**F**	**NG**

Inferring Meaning

A text does not always state everything directly. Sometimes you need to infer meaning by "reading between the lines." You can infer meaning by using what you already know about the topic, clues in the text, and common sense. For example, in Reading B, we know there were tire marks at the crime scene, so it is likely that the thief traveled by car.

INFERRING
MEANING

A. Look at some facts from Reading B. What can you infer?

1. There was no broken glass on the street.
   a. The thief broke the window from the inside.
   b. The thief broke the window from the outside.

2. The shoeprints were large.
   a. The thief was a man.
   b. The thief was a woman.

3. The space between shoeprints near the tire marks got farther apart.
   a. The thief was walking more slowly, and then stopping.
   b. The thief was walking faster, maybe running.

▲ **A police officer searches for fingerprints.**

INFERRING
MEANING

B. How sure are you of these things? Check (✓) the things you can infer from the passage. Compare your ideas with a partner and explain your reasons.

1. ☐ The crime happened at night.
2. ☐ The investigator will check the fingerprints of people who work in the store.
3. ☐ The thief had help from another person.
4. ☐ The hair belongs to the thief.
5. ☐ The thief was wearing expensive shoes.

CRITICAL THINKING Evaluating Evidence

▶ Imagine the following items are also found at the crime scene in Reading B. How helpful will they be for solving the crime? Rate each one from 1 (very useful) to 5 (not useful).

_____ a rock by the window   _____ a mark made with a glove

_____ a drop of blood near the window   _____ a drop of oil from the car

_____ a cellphone on the road outside   _____ a flashlight on the store floor

▶ Discuss your ideas with a partner.

COMPLETION   **A.** Complete the information. Circle the correct words.

We know that one of the best ways to
¹**catch** / **step** a thief is by collecting
fingerprints from a crime scene and then
²**comparing** / **stepping** them to others
with a computer. But how difficult is it to get
the prints?

Try this: Press a finger onto a drinking glass.
If your fingers are oily or wet, the print will
be better. Then cover the print and the
³**direction** / **space** around it with a small
amount of powder. You can use things you have in
your kitchen, such as flour or cocoa powder.

Now remove some of the powder with a small,
dry paintbrush until you see the print. Then
place some tape over the print. Take the tape
off and put it on a piece of paper. If ⁴**alone** /

Powder is used to cover the
pattern of the fingerprint so it
can be seen clearly.

possible, use colored paper. You should now see the fingerprint clearly.

DEFINITIONS   **B.** Complete the sentences. Circle the correct options.

1. If you are **alone**, you are with *no* / *one or more* other people.
2. You use your *hands* / *feet* to take a **step**.
3. An example of a **vehicle** is a *house* / *bus*.
4. The **direction** of a moving object is the *general line it follows* / *place it started from*.

WORD FORMS   **C.** The box below shows the different word forms of the word **possible**.
Complete the sentences using the words in the box.

possible (adj)   **possibly** (adv)   **possibility** (n)

1. There is a strong _____ that the thief is a woman.
2. The thief _____ left the scene in a large car.
3. It's _____ that no one will ever catch the thief.

72 Unit 5B

The flu virus affects millions of people around the world each year.

THE FLU VIRUS

BEFORE YOU WATCH

PREVIEWING **A.** Read the information. The words in **bold** appear in the video. Match each word with its definition.

Flu—or influenza—is a **virus** that you've probably had before. If you have the flu, you might have a fever, a headache, a cough, or a sore throat. Usually, you'll feel better after a few days, but some types of flu can be **deadly**. Flu can also **spread** very quickly and can affect a large number of people.

1. deadly •   • a. (n) a small living thing that makes you feel ill

2. spread •   • b. (adj) able to kill

3. virus •   • c. (v) to reach a larger area

DISCUSSION **B.** Discuss the questions below with a partner.

1. Can you remember the last time you had the flu? How did you feel?

2. What is the difference between the flu and a cold?

GIST   **A.** Watch the video. Complete the sentences by circling the correct options.

    1. Avian flu starts in *birds / pigs*.

    2. Swine flu starts in *birds / pigs*.

    3. Spanish flu started in *birds / pigs*.

DETAILS   **B.** Watch the video again. Complete the information using the numbers in the box. One is extra.

5,000   36,000   200,000   375,000   50 million

    1. Flu kills more than _____ people each year in the United States alone.

    2. Since 2004, scientists have identified more than _____ different flu viruses.

    3. Spanish flu killed _____ people between 1918 and 1919.

    4. In 2009, a type of swine flu affected _____ people.

CRITICAL THINKING Synthesizing Information   Look at the jobs in the box and answer the questions that follow. Compare your ideas with a partner and explain your reasons.

a. a scientist creating a flu medicine   b. a disease detective   c. a crime scene investigator

▶   Who do you think has the most interesting job? _____

▶   Who do you think has the most difficult job?   _____

▶   Who do you think has the most important job?   _____

VOCABULARY REVIEW

Do you remember the meanings of these words? Check (✓) the ones you know. Look back at the unit and review any words you're not sure of.

Reading A

☐ dangerous   ☐ dirty   ☐ expert*   ☐ ground

☐ illness   ☐ kill   ☐ list   ☐ touch

Reading B

☐ alone   ☐ catch   ☐ compare   ☐ direction

☐ possible   ☐ space   ☐ step   ☐ vehicle*

* Academic Word List

PLANTS AND TREES

A 4,000-year-old bristlecone pine tree in California, United States.

WARM UP

Discuss these questions with a partner.

1. Read the caption. What is special about this tree?

2. Why are trees important to our planet?

BEFORE YOU READ

DEFINITIONS **A.** Look at the photo and read the caption. Complete the definitions using the correct form of the words in **bold**.

1. If you _____ someone, you make them want to do something.

2. If you _____ a tree, you put it in the ground so it can grow.

SCANNING **B.** Scan the reading for numbers. What was Felix Finkbeiner's original tree-planting target? What is the target now?

> Felix Finkbeiner—aged 13 in this photo—encourages people around the world to plant more trees.

PLANTING
FOR THE PLANET

A   When he was nine years old, Felix Finkbeiner gave a class **presentation** on climate change. The young German spoke about deforestation[1] and its effect on the planet. At the end of his talk, he **challenged** the people of his country to help by planting one million trees. Nobody thought much would come of a nine-year-old's school project. Before he was 20, however, Finkbeiner's efforts had resulted in the planting of more than 14 billion trees around the world.

Der Steiger Award

At age 17, Finkbeiner gave this talk in Dortmund, Germany.

B   Finkbeiner and his **classmates** began the project—named "Plant-for-the-Planet"—by planting the first tree outside their school. Other schools followed the example, and **news** of the one-million challenge spread. As a result, Finkbeiner was asked to speak at the European Parliament. Other **invitations** soon followed, and when he was just 13, he spoke at a United Nations conference[2] in New York. "We cannot trust that adults alone will **save** our future," he said in the **speech**. "We have to take our future in our own hands."

C   Finkbeiner is now in his twenties, and Plant-for-the-Planet is an organization with around 70,000 **members**. It works to teach people about climate change and to encourage the planting of more trees. Germany's one millionth tree was planted long ago. The goal now is one trillion[3]—150 for every person on Earth.

D   Finkbeiner continues to give talks on climate change to world leaders. "I don't think we can give up on this generation of adults," he says, "and wait 20 or 30 years for our generation to come to power. We don't have that time. All we can do is push [current world leaders] in the right direction."

---

1 **Deforestation** is the cutting down of the world's trees and forests.
2 A **conference** is a large meeting of people.
3 A **trillion** is 1,000,000,000,000.

A. Choose the best answer for each question.

GIST

1. What is the reading mainly about?

    a. the problems deforestation can cause for our planet

    b. how planting trees can help the environment

    c. how a young person has made a big difference to the environment

PURPOSE

2. What is the purpose of paragraph B?

    a. to give an example of the challenges Finkbeiner faced

    b. to explain how Finkbeiner's project grew

    c. to describe Finkbeiner's personality

DETAIL

3. What is NOT true about Plant-for-the-Planet today?

    a. It teaches people about deforestation.

    b. It has many thousands of members.

    c. Its aim is to plant one billion trees.

∧ **A child plants a tree as part of the Plant-for-the-Planet project.**

REFERENCE

4. In paragraph C, what does the word *It* refer to?

    a. Plant-for-the-Planet

    b. Germany's one millionth tree

    c. climate change

PARAPHRASING

5. Which of the following is the best summary of Finkbeiner's quote in paragraph D?

    a. It will be easier to make changes when today's young people have more power.

    b. Young people today need to push those in power to make changes.

    c. Today's world leaders are a good example for younger generations to follow.

SCANNING

B. Write short answers to the questions below. Use words or numbers from the reading passage for each answer.

1. Who helped Finkbeiner plant his first tree?

_____

2. In which city did Finkbeiner speak to the United Nations?

_____

3. How many members does Plant-for-the-Planet have?

_____

Creating a Timeline of Events

When you read a text that has a number of different events, it can be useful to put them on a timeline. This helps you understand the order in which the events happened. Look carefully at words that signal sequence like *then, after, soon, when, now,* and *once.* But be careful, because events may not always appear in the passage in the order that they happened.

SCANNING   **A.** **Find and underline these events in Reading A.**

   a. Finkbeiner speaks to the United Nations.
   b. Finkbeiner challenges people in his country to plant a million trees.
   c. Other schools start to plant trees.
   d. Finkbeiner is asked to give a class presentation on climate change.
   e. Finkbeiner speaks to the European Parliament.
   f. Finkbeiner and his classmates plant a tree outside their school.

SEQUENCING   **B.** **Label the timeline with the events in activity A.**

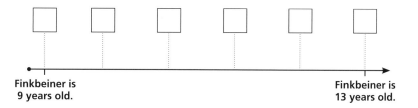

Finkbeiner is
9 years old.

Finkbeiner is
13 years old.

CRITICAL THINKING Justifying Opinions   Imagine you and your classmates accepted Felix Finkbeiner's challenge to plant trees. Where is a good place to plant trees in your area? Why? Note your ideas below. Then discuss with a partner.

Children in Germany taking part in Plant-for-the-Planet

COMPLETION **A.** Complete the information using the words in the box. Two words are extra.

challenge	invitations	members
news	save	speeches

Jadav Payeng lives in northeast India on the largest river island in the world. Since 1979, the river has slowly washed away much of the island. To help ¹_____ it, Payeng has planted tens of thousands of trees over the course of 30 years.

It all started when Payeng was in high school. He asked ²_____ of a local tribe if they could help with the island's problem. They advised him to plant trees and gave him 50 seeds. Forty years later, the forest stretches over more than five km^2.

∧ **Jadav Payeng, the "Forest Man of India"**

³_____ of Payeng's success spread. Now known as the "Forest Man of India," he works to educate others and has given many ⁴_____ across the country.

DEFINITIONS **B.** Complete the sentences. Circle the correct words.

1. Your **classmates** are people you go to *school / work* with.

2. When you give a **presentation**, you *speak / write* to a group of people.

3. If you **challenge** someone, you invite them to do a(n) *difficult / easy* task.

4. If someone gives you an **invitation**, they want you to *join / organize* an event.

WORD FORMS **C.** Some verbs can be made into nouns by adding *-ation* (e.g., **invite → invitation**). Write the noun form of these verbs. Check your spelling in a dictionary.

invite   → _____*invitation*_____   present → _____

transport → _____   educate → _____

prepare   → _____   inform   → _____

BEFORE YOU READ

PREVIEWING **A.** Look at the photo and read the caption. What does *carnivorous* mean? Check your ideas in a dictionary.

SKIMMING **B.** Do you know how Venus flytraps catch their food? Discuss with a partner. Skim the reading to check your ideas.

⌄ Venus flytraps are a species of carnivorous plant. They get most of their energy from catching and eating small insects.

FATAL ATTRACTION

A   A hungry fly speeds through a **forest**. It smells nectar[1] and lands on a green **leaf**. It starts to drink the sweet liquid. Suddenly, the fly's world turns green. The two sides of the leaf close against each other. Long green teeth **lock** together around it. The fly has been caught by a Venus flytrap. There is no escape.

B   The Venus flytrap is perhaps the most **famous** killer plant. However, scientists have only recently started to understand how it hunts and eats. After years of study, plant scientist Alexander Volkov believes he now knows the Venus flytrap's secret. "This," says Volkov, "is an **electrical** plant."

C   There are three small hairs **along** each of the Venus flytrap's two leaves. When an insect touches a hair, it creates an electrical signal in the leaf. The insect can continue feeding—for now. But if it touches another hair **within** 20 seconds, the trap snaps shut. This system allows the plant to tell the **difference** between a drop of water, for example, and a moving creature.

D   Once trapped, an insect has little chance of survival. Instead of nectar, the Venus flytrap now releases a different liquid—one that slowly eats away at the insect. Ten days later, almost nothing is left. The plant's leaves open again, and the Venus flytrap is ready for its next meal.

---

1 Many plants produce **nectar**, a liquid that insects feed on.

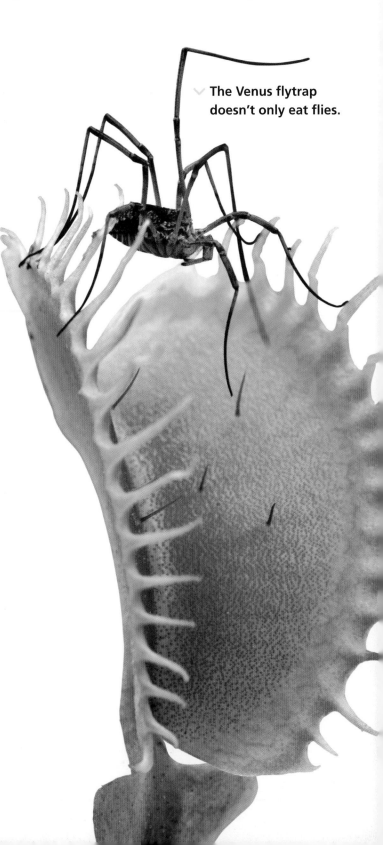

The Venus flytrap doesn't only eat flies.

KILLER PLANTS

There are around 700 species of killer plants around the world.
Here are some of the most deadly.

∧ Sundews catch insects using a sticky
liquid on the end of long hairs.

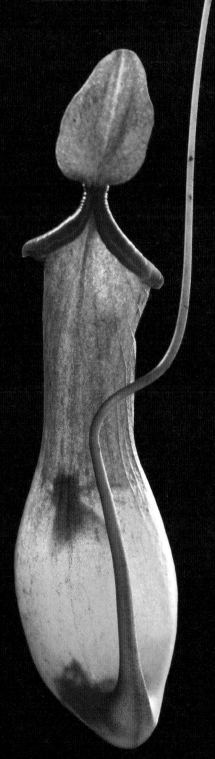

∨ Pitcher plants have
long, tubelike
leaves into which
insects fall and die.

∧ A butterwort's leaves are covered with
tiny, gluey hairs that trap small insects.

A. Choose the best answer for each question.

GIST **1.** What is the reading mainly about?

    a. plants that catch and eat insects
    b. plants that are dangerous to humans
    c. how plants create nectar for insects

DETAIL **2.** What is NOT true about the Venus flytrap?

    a. It can make two different kinds of liquid.
    b. It uses electrical signals.
    c. Its trap closes very slowly.

PURPOSE **3.** What is the purpose of paragraph C?

    a. to explain how the Venus flytrap works
    b. to describe different types of carnivorous plants
    c. to describe an experiment carried out on a plant

INFERENCE **4.** Around how many flies could a Venus flytrap eat in one month?

    a. 3 or 4
    b. between 20 and 30
    c. more than 100

Some pitcher plants are large enough to catch and eat small animals like frogs and mice.

DETAIL **5.** Which plant does not use hairs to catch insects?

    a. the sundew
    b. the butterwort
    c. the pitcher plant

INFERENCE **B.** Which of the following would cause the Venus flytrap to close? Check (✓) all that apply.

    a. ☐ A single drop of water touches a hair on a leaf.

    b. ☐ A fly touches a hair on a leaf. One minute later, it touches another hair.

    c. ☐ A fly touches a hair on a leaf. A few seconds later, a drop of water falls and touches a different hair.

    d. ☐ A small fly lands on a leaf. It drinks nectar without touching any hairs.

    e. ☐ Two small flies land on a leaf. One touches a hair. Immediately after, the other fly touches a different hair.

Understanding a Process

A process is a series of events or steps. To fully understand a process, it's important to identify the sequence of the individual events. A useful way to show the events and their relationship is to list them in a diagram.

ANALYZING **A.** Look back at Reading B. Underline any signal words or phrases that indicate a sequence (see Reading Skill 6A).

UNDERSTANDING A PROCESS **B.** How does a Venus flytrap catch its prey? Put the events in order (a–g) in the diagram.

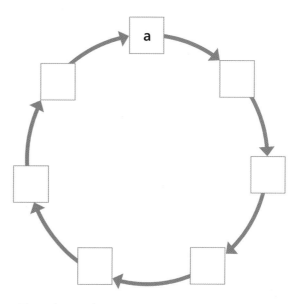

a. The plant releases nectar.
b. The trap reopens.
c. A fly lands on the plant's leaf.
d. The trap closes.
e. The plant releases a liquid to break down the fly.
f. The fly touches a second hair.
g. The fly touches a hair.

CRITICAL THINKING Applying Ideas

▶ In what ways is a Venus flytrap similar to an animal? Note some ideas below.

_____

_____

▶ Compare your ideas with a partner.

DEFINITIONS **A.** Read the information. Match the correct form of each word in **red** with its definition.

Like the Venus flytrap, the sundew is a killer plant. Sundews can be found in swamps and **forests** around the world. There are many types of sundews, ranging in size from a small coin to a large bush.

The sundew produces a sticky liquid that covers the hairs on its **leaves**. When an insect lands on the plant in search

∧ **The sticky hairs on the leaf of a sundew plant**

of food, it gets stuck. As the insect tries to get free, more hairs stick to it. Some types of sundew are even able to curl their leaves over the insect and **lock** the unlucky creature **within**.

1. _____: inside

2. _____: a large group of trees

3. _____: to hold together tightly

4. _____: the flat (often green) part of a plant

WORDS IN CONTEXT **B.** Complete the sentences. Circle the correct options.

1. If there is a **difference** between two things, they are *not the same* / *the same*.

2. A *bed* / *television* is an example of an **electrical** item.

3. If something is **famous**, *few* / *many* people know about it.

4. You can walk **along** a *city* / *road*.

COLLOCATIONS **C.** The verbs *make* and *tell* are often used with the noun **difference**. Complete the sentences by circling the correct words.

1. Small changes to your diet can *make* / *tell* a big difference to your health.

2. Most people can't *make* / *tell* the difference between my twin daughters.

3. I've been waiting for three hours. Another 10 minutes won't *make* / *tell* any difference.

∨ Giant sequoia trees in Yosemite National Park, United States

GIANTS OF THE FOREST

BEFORE YOU WATCH

PREVIEWING   **A.** The words in the box appear in the video. Complete the sentences using the words. Use a dictionary to help.

bark	branches	roots	trunk

1. A tree's _____ is its thickest part. It gives the tree its shape and strength.

2. The _____ of a tree grow below the ground. They stop the tree from falling down and also take food and water from the earth.

3. Most trees are covered in _____. This protects it from animals and the environment.

4. The _____ of a tree are the parts that grow outwards. They are often covered in leaves.

PREVIEWING   **B.** Find examples of each word in activity A in the photo above.

GIST **A.** Watch the video. Why do giant sequoia trees grow so big? Note three reasons below.

1. _____ 2. _____ 3. _____

DETAILS **B.** Watch the video again. Complete the notes about General Sherman using numbers from the video.

General Sherman

- over ^{1}_____ years old

- over ^{2}_____ meters tall

- first branches start growing at ^{3}_____ meters

- distance around trunk over ^{4}_____ meters

CRITICAL THINKING Applying Ideas The video says that giant sequoias "are one of the largest living things on Earth." What do you think are the other largest living things? Note some ideas below. Then discuss with a partner.

_____

_____

VOCABULARY REVIEW

Do you remember the meanings of these words? Check (✓) the ones you know. Look back at the unit and review any words you're not sure of.

Reading A

☐ challenge* ☐ classmate ☐ invitation ☐ member

☐ news ☐ presentation ☐ save ☐ speech

Reading B

☐ along ☐ difference ☐ electrical ☐ famous

☐ forest ☐ leaf ☐ lock ☐ within

* Academic Word List

Photo and Illustration Credits

Text Credits

Acknowledgments

The Authors and Publisher would like to thank the following teaching professionals for their valuable feedback during the development of the series.

Akiko Hagiwara, Tokyo University of Pharmacy and Life Sciences; **Albert Lehner**, University of Fukui; **Alexander Cameron**, Kyushu Sangyo University; **Amira Traish**, University of Sharjah; **Andrés López**, Colégio José Max León; **Andrew Gallacher**, Kyushu Sangyo University; **Angelica Hernandez**, Liceo San Agustin; **Angus Painter**, Fukuoka University; **Anouchka Rachelson**, Miami Dade College; **Ari Hayakawa**, Aoyama Gakuin University; **Atsuko Otsuki**, Senshu University; **Ayako Hisatsune**, Kanazawa Institute of Technology; **Bogdan Pavliy**, Toyama University of International Studies; **Braden Chase**, The Braden Chase Company; **Brian J. Damm**, Kanda Institute of Foreign Languages; **Carol Friend**, Mercer County Community College; **Catherine Yu**, CNC Language School; **Chad Godfrey**, Saitama Medical University; **Cheng-hao Weng**, SMIC Private School; **Chisako Nakamura**, Ryukoku University; **Chiyo Myojin**, Kochi University of Technology; **Chris Valvona**, Okinawa Christian College; **Claire DeFord**, Olympic College; **Davi Sukses**, Sutomo 1; **David Farnell**, Fukuoka University; **David Johnson**, Kyushu Sangyo University; **Debbie Sou**, Kwong Tai Middle School; **Devin Ferreira**, University of Central Florida; **Eden Kaiser**, Framingham State University; **Ellie Park**, CNC Language School; **Elvis Bartra García**, Corporación Educativa Continental; **Emiko Yamada**, Westgate Corporation; **Eri Tamura**, Ishikawa Prefectural University; **Fadwa Sleiman**, University of Sharjah; **Frank Gutsche**, Tohoku University; **Frank Lin**, Guangzhou Tufu Culture; **Gavin Young**, Iwate University; **Gerry Landers**, GA Tech Language Institute; **Ghada Ahmed**, University of Bahrain; **Grace Choi**, Grace English School; **Greg Bevan**, Fukuoka University; **Gregg McNabb**, Shizuoka Institute of Science and Technology; **Helen Roland**, Miami Dade College; **Hiroshi Ohashi**, Kyushu University; **Hiroyo Yoshida**, Toyo University; **Hojin Song**, GloLink Education; **Jackie Bae**, Plato Language School; **Jade Wong**, Belilios Public School; **James McCarron**, Chiba University; **Jane Kirsch**, INTO George Mason University; **Jenay Seymore**, Hong Ik University; **John Appleby**, Kanda Institute of Foreign Languages; **John Nevara**, Kagoshima University; **Jonathan Bronson**, Approach International Student Center; **Joseph Zhou**, UUabc; **Josh Brunotte**, Aichi Prefectural University; **Junjun Zhou**, Menaul School; **Kaori Yamamoto; Katarina Zorkic**, Rosemead College; **Keiko Miyagawa**, Meiji University; **Kevin Tang**, Ritsumeikan Asia Pacific University; **Kieran Julian**, Kanda Institute of Foreign Languages; **Kim Kawashima**, Olympic College; **Kyle Kumataka**, Ritsumeikan Asia Pacific University; **Kyosuke Shimamura**, Kurume University; **Lance Stilp**, Ritsumeikan Asia Pacific University; **Li Zhaoli**, Weifang No.7 Middle School; **Liza Armstrong**, University of Missouri; **Lucas Pignolet**, Ritsumeikan Asia Pacific University; **Luke Harrington**, Chiba University; **M. Lee**, KCC; **Maiko Berger**, Ritsumeikan Asia Pacific University; **Mandy Kan**, CNEC Christian College; **Mari Nakamura**, English Square; **Masako Kikukawa**, Doshisha University; **Matthew Fraser**, Westgate Corporation; **Mayuko Matsunuma**, Seijo University; **Michiko Imai**, Aichi University; **Mei-ho Chiu**, Soochow University; **Melissa Potts**, ELS Berkeley; **Monica Espinoza**, Torrance Adult School; **Ms. Manassara Riensumettharadol**, Kasetsart University; **My Uyen Tran**, Ho Chi Minh City University of Foreign Languages and Information Technology; **Narahiko Inoue**, Kyushu University; **Neil Witkin**, Kyushu Sangyo University; **Noriko Tomioka**, Kwansei University; **Olesya Shatunova**, Kanagawa University; **Patricia Fiene**, Midwestern Career College; **Patricia Nation**, Miami Dade College; **Patrick John Johnston**, Ritsumeikan Asia Pacific University; **Paula Snyder**, University of Missouri-Columbia; **Paul Hansen**, Hokkaido University; **Ping Zhang**, Beijing Royal School; **Reiko Kachi**, Aichi University / Chukyo University; **Robert Dykes**, Jin-ai University; **Rosanna Bird**, Approach International Student Center; **Ryo Takahira**, Kurume Fusetsu High School; **Samuel Taylor**, Kyushu Sangyo University; **Sandra Stein**, American University of Kuwait; **Sanooch Nathalang**, Thammasat University; **Sara Sulko**, University of Missouri; **Serena Lo**, Wong Shiu Chi Secondary School; **Shin Okada**, Osaka University; **Silvana Carlini**, Colégio Agostiniano Mendel; **Silvia Yafai**, ADVETI: Applied Tech High School; **Stella Millikan**, Fukuoka Women's University; **Summer Webb**, University of Colorado Boulder; **Susumu Hiramatsu**, Okayama University; **Suzanne Littlewood**, Zayed University; **Takako Kuwayama**, Kansai University; **Takashi Urabe**, Aoyama-Gakuin University; **Teo Kim**, OROMedu; **Tim Chambers; Toshiya Tanaka**, Kyushu University; **Trevor Holster**, Fukuoka University; **Wakako Takinami**, Tottori University; **Wayne Malcolm**, Fukui University of Technology; **Wendy Wish**, Valencia College; **Xiaoying Zhan**, Bejing Royal Foreign Language School; **Xingwu Chen**, Xueersi-TAL; **Yin Wang**, TAL Education Group; **Yohei Murayama**, Kagoshima University; **Yoko Sakurai**, Aichi University; **Yoko Sato**, Tokyo University of Agriculture and Technology; **Yoon-Ji Ahn**, Daks Education; **Yu-Lim Im**, Daks Education; **Yuriko Ueda**, Ryukoku University; **Yvonne Hodnett**, Australian College of Kuwait; **Yvonne Johnson**, UWCSEA Dover; **Zhang Lianzhong**, Beijing Foreign Studies University

GLOSSARY

These words are used in *Reading Explorer* to describe various reading and critical thinking skills.

Analyze	to study a text in detail, e.g., to identify key points, similarities, and differences
Apply	to think about how an idea might be useful in other ways, e.g., solutions to a problem
Classify	to arrange things in groups or categories, based on their characteristics
Evaluate	to examine different sides of an issue, e.g., reasons for and against something
Infer	to "read between the lines"—information the writer expresses indirectly
Interpret	to think about what a writer means by a certain phrase or expression
Justify	to give reasons for a personal opinion, belief, or decision
Rank	to put things in order based on criteria, e.g., size or importance
Reflect	to think deeply about what a writer is saying and how it compares with your own views
Relate	to consider how ideas in a text connect with your own personal experience
Scan	to look through a text to find particular words or information
Skim	to look at a text quickly to get an overall understanding of its main idea
Summarize	to give a brief statement of the main points of a text
Synthesize	to use information from more than one source to make a judgment or comparison

INDEX OF EXAM QUESTION TYPES

The activities in *Reading Explorer, Third Edition* provide comprehensive practice of several question types that feature in standardized tests such as TOEFL® and IELTS.

Common Question Types	IELTS	TOEFL®	Page(s)
Multiple choice (main idea, detail, reference, inference, vocabulary, paraphrasing)	✓	✓	11, 16, 25, 30, 38, 44, 53, 58, 65, 70, 78, 84
Completion (notes, diagram, chart)	✓		20, 48, 74, 79, 88
Completion (summary)	✓	✓	11, 53, 65
Short answer	✓		16, 78
Matching headings / information	✓		25, 30, 34, 38, 58, 62
True / False / Not Given	✓		70
Rhetorical purpose		✓	25, 30, 38, 66, 78, 84

The following tips will help you become a more successful reader.

1 Preview the text

Before you start reading a text, it's important to have some idea of the overall topic. Look at the title, photos, captions, and any maps or infographics. Skim the text quickly, and scan for any key words before reading in detail (see pages 8 and 14).

2 Use vocabulary strategies

Here are some strategies to use if you find a word or phrase you're not sure of:

- **Use context** to guess the meaning of new words.
- **Look at word parts** (e.g., affixes) to work out what a word means (see page 45).
- **Look for definitions** of new words within the reading passage itself.
- **Use a dictionary** if you need, but be careful to identify the correct definition (see page 39).

3 Take notes

Note-taking helps you identify the main ideas and details within a text. It also helps you stay focused while reading. Try different ways of organizing your notes, and decide on a method that best suits you.

4 Infer information

Not everything is stated directly within a text. Use your own knowledge, and clues in the text, to make your own inferences and "read between the lines" (see page 71).

5 Make connections

As you read, look for words that help you understand how different ideas connect. For example:

- words that show the **order of events** (see page 79)
- words that explain **cause-and-effect** relationships
- words that introduce **examples**

6 Read critically

Ask yourself questions as you read a text. For example, if the author presents a point of view, is enough supporting evidence provided? Is the evidence reliable? Does the author give a balanced argument?

7 Create a summary

Creating a summary is a great way to check your understanding of a text. It also makes it easier to remember the main points. You can summarize in different ways based on the type of text. For example:

- **timelines** (see page 79)
- **T-charts**
- **concept maps**
- **visual summaries** (see page 88)